To my lovely Patsy Christmas 1982
with love
Mother Bingham

Modern Acts of the Holy Spirit

R. PAUL CAUDILL

MODERN ACTS OF THE HOLY SPIRIT

BROADMAN PRESS
Nashville, Tennessee

Scriptures marked ASV are from the American Standard Version of the Bible. ©1901, Thomas Nelson & Sons.

Scriptures marked RSV are from the Revised Standard Version of the Bible, copyrighted 1946, 1952, ©1971, 1973.

Scriptures marked Williams are from *The New Testament, a Translation in the Language of the People* by Charles B. Williams. Copyright 1937 and 1966. Moody Press, Moody Bible Institute of Chicago. Used by permission.

Scriptures marked Phillips are reprinted with permission of Macmillan Publishing Co., Inc. from J. B. Phillips: *The New Testament in Modern English,* Revised Edition. © J. B. Phillips 1958, 1960, 1972.

Scriptures marked NEB are from *The New English Bible.* Copyright ©The Delegates of the Oxford University Press and the Syndics of the Cambridge University Press, 1961, 1970. Reprinted by permission.

Scriptures marked TCNT are from the *Twentieth Century New Testament,* The Moody Bible Institute.

Scriptures marked AT are the author's translation.

Dewey Decimal Classification: 231.3
Subject heading: HOLY SPIRIT
Library of Congress Catalog Number: 81-67992
Printed in the United States of America

Dedicated to
the Person of the Holy Spirit,

the Christian's Helper and Friend,
who continues
to convict the world of sin,
and of righteousness,
and of the judgment;
and to teach us all things,
guide us unto all truth,
and bring to our remembrance
the sayings of Jesus.

Foreword

Only a pastor with long experience in every kind of life situation who was, at the same time, thoroughly at home in his Greek New Testament, could have written such a book as this. This is an exceedingly rare combination, and it makes possible one of the most exciting books on the Holy Spirit you will ever have the opportunity to read.

Dr. Caudill is a consummate storyteller, and he traces the power and presence of the Holy Spirit in every kind of human situation, from the very dramatic to the ordinary experiences of life. In the mending of a broken home and the healing of a bitter feud, through the glorious experience of personal salvation and the spiritual renewal of the church, in the loneliness of long illness and the shattering time of grief, he portrays the "modern acts" of the Holy Spirit in forceful and direct language. The experiences are related with such gripping power that the reader will be unable to put the book down. Every story will touch someone at the point of an experience in his life, and the ministry of the Holy Spirit will become more real in the life of the reader as he sees the way in which "God is working through everything for good" (see Rom. 8:28).

In a way that is unique in my experience, Part II of the book presents a clear and readable summary of the New Testament teachings about the person and work of the Holy Spirit. Here the author's profound grasp of the Greek text of the New Testament shines through each interpretation; yet it is written in plain and direct language for all to understand. It is a short course in "the biblical theology of the Holy Spirit," and it will enrich the life of anyone who takes the time to read it carefully. Altogether, it is one of the finest examples of relating the Bible to life that I have ever seen. Only the Holy Spirit could have inspired such a moving witness to his own life and work.

Wayne Ward
The Southern Baptist Theological Seminary

Preface

This book has to do with the Holy Spirit. In Part I, I have attempted to set down faithfully, in descriptive narration, some of the acts of the Holy Spirit which I have witnessed in contemporary society during my ministry, which began with ordination on August 9, 1925. Each act of the Spirit, as recorded, has to do with a life situation such as the average person may experience in today's world. Each experience is related just as it took place. The stories are not embellished, and each wears the garments of integrity. Only the names of persons and places have been changed, at times, for the sake of anonymity.

Doubtless each Christian reader has had experiences in life when there was an unusual consciousness of the Spirit's presence. My experience, therefore, as set forth in the account of "modern acts" of the Holy Spirit which I have witnessed, is not necessarily unique. For wherever there is a viable relationship between believers and the Heavenly Father, and where those believers have a knowledgeable relationship with the character and work of the Holy Spirit, they have been aware of the presence and work of the Spirit.

Part II consists of brief notes concerning some of the biblical teachings that relate to the person, the presence, and the power of the Holy Spirit, and how we as believers may come to know him and experience his presence in our lives. Obviously, the notes are not intended to be a comprehensive treatment of the biblical doctrine of the Holy Spirit; but for those who would grow in their knowledge concerning the Holy Spirit and in their personal relationships with the Spirit, it is hoped that the study, brief and partial as it is, may be helpful.

I suggest that the reader might well seek a time and place where there is reasonable quiet and freedom from interruption to read this book. This is highly desirable for all seasons of meditation and study where the deeper aspects of the Christian life are involved.

I am deeply appreciative for the assistance of Dr. Wayne Ward in reading the manuscript, for his constructive criticism of it, and for his great kindness in writing the Foreword. I also thank my gifted secretary, Mrs. Eugenia Price, for her meticulous care in typing and proofreading the manuscript. My lasting gratitude also goes out to my beloved wife Fern for her tireless hours spent in reading and proofreading the manuscript, and for valuable suggestions here and there.

If the sharing of these experiences, along with the brief "Notes on the Holy Spirit," serves to deepen the consciousness of the Spirit's presence in a single life, and leads one person into a closer walk with God, my effort in the writing of this book will not have been in vain.

R. Paul Caudill

Table of Contents

PART I
Modern Acts of the Holy Spirit

PART II
Notes on the Holy Spirit

PART I
Modern Acts of the Holy Spirit

1

The Holy Spirit and Children

"What age should children be when they are received as candidates for baptism and church membership?" I was asked this question only recently and at least twenty times over the years. This is a question that has plagued many minds, especially those of evangelicals, throughout the years.

My answer to the question was, "You cannot make this important determination by the age level. It simply can't be answered that way, for the simple fact that some children are far more advanced in their spiritual understanding at the age of seven or eight than others may be at fourteen or fifteen." This is because of the kind of instruction the child has received and the kind of life-style with which the child has been surrounded.

This type of question about the ability of a child to respond effectually to the claims of Christ was present even among the disciples, as Matthew records; for he tells us that when they brought children to Jesus so that he might put his hands upon them and pray, his disciples rebuked them for doing so.

Then it was that Jesus uttered words that helped to transform the whole concept of the ancient world concerning the worth and the place of the little child in society at large.

That concept, in the days of Jesus, needed desperately to be changed, for a little child, up until then, had little worth in the eyes of men. Infant exposure, for instance, was very common among Gentiles. The pagan mind thought nothing of taking an unwanted child and placing it out in the edge of the forest for the wild beasts to devour. That is a terrible thing to say, but that is exactly what was done. For example, there is an old papyrus letter written by an Egyptian soldier, Hilarion, to his wife, Ali. Hilarion had been home for a stay and then returned to active duty in the field. "If by all means you bear a child, if it is a male, let it live. If it is a female, cast it out."

We know from ancient history that among Gentiles child sacrifice was a common practice. One has only to look at the findings of the excavations of such walled cities as Jericho to find the fragmented remains of the bones of babies who were sacrificed at the laying of the foundations. The teachings of Jesus opposed such a baneful practice, for it was he who placed his hands upon the children brought to him and said, "Suffer the little children, and forbid them not, to come unto me: for to such belongeth the kingdom of heaven" (Matt. 19:14, ASV).

On the mission fields, evangelical missionaries have been slow to receive children as candidates for baptism because of the total absence of religious instruction in their early lives. Being wholly unacquainted with the way, the truth, and the life of Jesus, they are not prepared for the decisions involving their whole life-style forever. There have to be extended seasons of instruction and preparation.

But what of the presence and the power of the Holy Spirit with regard to little children? Is a small child of six, seven, or eight years able to comprehend the Spirit's presence and to respond effectually to the Spirit's pleading?

My own view in the matter was influenced, markedly, by two experiences that came to me in the pastorate. One of them involved our firstborn daughter, Netta Sue. The other involved Carol McCall, the young daughter of Dr. and Mrs. John W. McCall. May I share these two experiences with you?

One morning following the worship service at the First Baptist Church of Carrollton, Kentucky, where I was a student pastor, my wife and I and Netta Sue had just returned to the parsonage where we soon were to have the noonday meal.

While Fern was preparing the meal, I came in and sat down in a comfortable chair by the old Crosley radio, thinking I might pick up a bit of news or hear a musical program that would offer relaxation. I had hardly sat down in the chair when Netta Sue came, climbed up into my lap, and, in a more or less nonchalant manner, said to me, "Daddy, I have something I want to talk to you about, but I guess we better wait until after dinner."

Replying to her, I said, "That will be fine, Netta Sue—we will talk after we have had our dinner." At the moment, I had no more idea what Netta Sue wanted to talk about than a man in the moon would have had! She was so very young, it did not once occur to me that she wanted to talk about becoming a Christian. After all, she spoke in such a matter-of-fact way that I thought she might be wanting to talk about school, for she was in the first grade.

After a delectable meal, I came back and sat down in the same chair to relax for a few moments before going out on some afternoon calls. Almost immediately, Netta Sue came and climbed up in my lap again. This time there was a very somber look on her face. She looked up at me, paused, and then threw her arms around my neck and began to cry. Wondering what in the world might be the matter, I was on the point of asking her what was wrong when she broke in on my thoughts, saying, "Daddy, I have something that I want to talk to you about, but I'm afraid!"

"Afraid!" said I. "Afraid to talk to your father? How can that be? You should not be afraid to talk to your father about anything in the world, for you know how much I love you, and always will! You can talk to me about anything . . . anything!"

Then, looking up into my eyes, she said to me in a quiet manner, "I want to give my heart to Jesus! I want to be a Christian! I want to follow him as long as I live!"

Netta Sue was well-acquainted with my manner of receiving young people into the church. She had doubtless heard me say, again and again, "Is this decision that you are making, this decision to follow Jesus, to be for your whole life? Do you purpose to follow him so long as you live . . . never turning back for anything, for anybody?"

Her words came to me, I must confess, as a great surprise, for she was just approaching her seventh birthday. Of course, I had always looked upon her as being a bright, and at times almost precocious, child. So often she spoke on matters as an adult would speak.

For months, at the worship services, I had noticed how intensely she listened to my words as I preached. Sometimes on Sunday mornings, she would sit in the choir beside a deacon, Mr. Pleas Walters, the man from whom we bought our groceries, and whom she liked very much. Mr. Walters had a way with children, and Netta Sue had asked her mother if she might sit by him in the choir and sing with him. Brother Pleas seemed flattered to have her by his side, and so it was not an uncommon thing to see the little one sitting there beside him on the end seat of the back row where she had a good view of the pulpit as her father spoke, listening intently.

Upon hearing her words, I pulled her little arms loose from around my neck, for she was still clutching me tightly with her arms. I lifted her out on my knees so I had a good view of her face, and could talk to her directly.

Immediately I said to her, "Why, that's wonderful, Netta Sue; you can make your decision to follow Jesus right this very moment."

Then for a while I spoke to her concerning what a decision to follow Jesus means. I explained to her how Jesus said that those who follow him must repent and believe (see Mark 1:15).

Very carefully, I tried to explain the meaning of repentance, and how it calls for a change in the way one thinks and feels and acts, not only with reference to Jesus but also with regard to the people with whom one lives and works and plays. I tried to explain faith, and how one believes in the Lord Jesus.

At length, I endeavored to interpret for her the meaning of sin, explaining to her that Jesus came into the world to save us from our sins. I told her how the Bible tells us that we have all sinned and fallen short of God's purpose for us in life (Rom. 3:23). I also explained to her Paul's words in Romans 6:23 which tell us that "the wages of sin is death" whereas "the gift of God is eternal life." Endeavoring to make clear to her the real meaning of sin, I explained how, as the Bible tells us, it means "to miss the mark," the mark that God has for one in life. I told her how it is somewhat like the archer who draws the bow and lets the arrow fly—only to miss his mark. I told her how sin is simply going against God and his commands . . . that one who sins is a rebel, rebelling against God's ways for us in life.

After no little dialogue between us, in which I endeavored to give her every opportunity to ask questions, and then to answer them, I said to her, "Do you feel that there have been times in your life when you have sinned . . . when you have done things that the Heavenly Father wouldn't approve of?" Immediately she answered, "Yes, I have; I know I have." I suppose at the moment she was thinking about some little acts of disobedience in relation to her parents, for there had been a time or two when she had not cooperated with her mother and me as she might have done.

On one occasion, for instance, we were planning to drive from Carrollton to Cincinnati—a distance of fifty-two miles—to meet her grandmother, who was coming to us for a visit. But that morning she had exercised her independence too much and had overtly disobeyed us. It was not a big thing, but it was quite important in the matter of a child-parent relationship.

(In disciplining a child, I have never felt that it was wise for a parent to threaten to do this or that to a child but simply to give the child the instruction that is needed, or the commands—if you want to put it like that. Then if the child refuses to respond, whatever course of reproof the occasion demands must be taken.)

As we began to dress for the trip (for we had intended to make quite a day of it), I turned and said to Netta Sue, "Netta Sue, you will not go with us to Cincinnati today!" She seemed utterly dumbfounded at such a word. She only looked at me in amazement as if to say, "Well, why? Why am I not going?"

Quietly, I told her that she had been disobedient and un-cooperative that morning, and we felt that this was something that should not go by unnoticed. She would therefore remain at home with the maid and have time to think things over while we were gone. Maybe on our return, she would feel different about her responses to her parents' wishes.

Going off to Cincinnati without her, our firstborn and only child, was about the most difficult thing I suppose we ever did. It was an extremely difficult decision to make, but once we made it, we did not relent.

Upon our return, I recall vividly how joyful Netta Sue was. There was no pouting, no trace of unhappiness to be found in her face, and from that day on, there were few problems of discipline with her.

After Netta Sue told me that she knew there had been times when she had sinned, I remarked to her, "Yes, you understand, don't you? For the Bible says that children are to obey their parents in the Lord, because this is right, and you can recall some times in the past when you did not obey, can't you?"

Then I went on to say to her, "We will have a prayer together now, and if this is in your heart to do, you can yield your life to Jesus completely at this time."

After the prayer, she looked up inquiringly and said, "Now, when can I be baptized?"

In my reply to her, I did not intend to be evasive; I merely wanted to delay the matter for a time until I could give her further instruction. "We will talk about that now, Dear," I said, "but first I want you to understand fully the meaning of baptism and church membership, and I don't think we have talked enough about that yet.

"Being baptized and joining the church does not save you, for that is not the meaning of salvation. You are saved when you turn to Jesus, as I think you have done today, and when you resolve, with a repentant heart, to follow him forever as your Savior and Lord."

Then she said to me, "But why do you want me to wait to be baptized, Daddy? Are you afraid that I will not hold out?"

"No, it is not quite that, Dear," I replied. "I merely want to be sure that you have understanding, for this is part of the greatest step in life that you will ever take."

A few weeks later I was called to be pastor of the First Baptist Church of Augusta, Georgia, and we had come to our last Sunday at Carrollton. I had just delivered the morning sermon and extended the invitation. There was a response of some twelve or more individuals, both youth and adults, who came forward for baptism and church membership.

On that particular morning, Netta Sue was in the choir, sitting by deacon Pleas Walters. (Her mother was at home with her newborn baby brother.) I do not think that my eye turned toward her a single time as I preached. I had assumed that we would talk further about the matter before she presented herself to the church for baptism.

To my surprise, Netta Sue also came forward on the invitation and, standing directly in front of me and looking me straight in the eye, extended her right hand and said, "I want to follow Jesus and be baptized!"

Without further delay, I received her along with the others who came for baptism but stated to the congregation that I would prefer to baptize her on the following Sunday which would mark the beginning of my ministry in Augusta, Georgia.

On the first Sunday there, I led her down into the baptismal waters—the first one to be baptized under my ministry there.

More than forty years have passed since that happy event took place, but in all of the years, I have never for an instant doubted the genuineness of her experience in Christ. And nothing has happened in her life, since that experience, to cast doubtful shadows over the genuineness of her conversion and the faithfulness of her life as a follower of Christ. I have always felt that I had as soon have her conversion experience as my own, and through her I came to have a new understanding about the ability of little children to perceive the true meaning of conversion, of baptism, and of church membership.

The other experience, that of the conversion of young Carol McCall, was no less convincing. Let me briefly share with you what took place on the morning of her conversion, and what has taken place in the years that followed that eventful hour in her life.

Carol had been associated with the First Baptist Church of Memphis since the day she was born. Her name was entered in the Cradle Roll Department at the time of her birth, and at the earliest day, her father and mother brought her to Sunday School where she was tenderly placed, along with other little ones, in the church nursery that provided excellent care, not only during the Sunday School hour but during the worship service.

Her parents were devout in their Christian relationship, both to each other and to the church. Her father was a deacon, and her mother an elect lady of the church. Her maternal and paternal grandparents were also devoted to the church. All members of the family, on both sides of the house, were devout and faithful in their loyalties to Christ and to the church. They were people who participated regularly in all the activities of the church. They were there at Sunday School and at both of the worship services on Sunday. They were there at the midweek hour of worship. They took part in the meetings of the Brotherhood and Missionary Society. They were simply "church people" in the fullest sense of the word.

Little Carol's associations with the church, therefore, were as normal to her young mind as her associations with her home, for the church and the home were equally a part of her life experiences.

On the way to church on this particular morning, Carol related to her parents her desire to unite with the church and to be baptized. She told them she wanted to become a Christian—to become a follower of Jesus, and she wanted to start "today."

The father, realizing how young she was (only six years of age at the time), counseled with her (as he afterward told me), saying, "Well that is fine, Carol, but don't you think you should wait until the pastor has had a chance to talk with you and you with him? He always likes to talk with children before they take this great step that you want to take today."

Dr. McCall later confided that throughout the hour of worship he prayed constantly that if Carol's impulse were of the Lord and it was his time for her to make her decision that my sermon might have, in at least a portion of it, a message directly related to little children. In my sermon, he later reminded me, I did just that. I paused to speak a word directly to little children, acquainting them with the way of salvation in terms that a child could understand.

At First Baptist, Memphis, we did not have a separate worship service for children. Through the years, I encouraged the parents to bring their children into the sanctuary with them and sit together as family groups during the worship service when the children became too old for care in the nursery and Cradle Roll departments of the church. I made it a point to let the parents know that having small children in the congregation would in no way distract me from the delivery of my message. I explained to them that all the while the children would be learning in a way undreamed of by their elders.

So Carol had been coming into the main sanctuary with her parents for more than a year.

At the time of invitation on that unforgettable morning, Carol turned to her parents and said, "I've got to go, for Jesus is calling me—I have to go!" And with that, without allowing time for restraint on the part of her parents, Carol broke away from them and came marching down the aisle of the First Baptist Church. I can see her now as she came hastily forward to where I was standing, and I recall to this day the sincere look in her eyes as she grasped my hand and told me that she wanted to follow Jesus and be baptized.

Having had a similar experience with my own daughter, it was not difficult for me to realize that here was another work of the Holy Spirit—a genuine conversion wrought by the hand of God!

It was my privilege to continue to serve as Carol's pastor and see her come to the years of young womanhood. I watched her as a teenager at hours of worship, at church camp, in the halls of the church—in and out of season—and always I beheld in her the gentle graces of true Christian character.

Off to college she went, and from college she returned, the same girl that she was before—noble, virtuous, and upright in all her ways.

She stood before me at the marriage altar when she was wed to a Christian young man who was soon to become a physician, Greer Richardson. In the intervening years, three children have come into the home where they will be reared in the same atmosphere of love and faithful devotion to Christ and his church which Carol experienced in her own home. In the years that have followed I have felt, again and again, that I could hardly desire to see a more genuine conversion or a nobler exercise of life under the guiding hands of the Holy Spirit.

2

Faith at Death's Door

Early one weekday morning our residence telephone rang, and the disturbed voice of a nurse at John Gaston Hospital said, "Dr. Caudill, can you come to the hospital immediately? We need you!"

I had been out of bed only a few moments and was not yet fully dressed. I replied, "Yes, I will be there just as soon as I can dress and drive down."

The nurse added, "Come to Ward C on the second floor of John Gaston. We've got a bad situation, and we need your help."

A man had been brought to the emergency room of the hospital. A short time before, he had swallowed a large dose of rat poison in a suicide attempt. The patient had been brought to the hospital too late for any effective measures to be taken, but they did the best they could for him and sent him to Ward C to die. The patient's body had retained the poison too long, and it was obvious to the doctors that the time would be short.

Soon after the patient was brought to Ward C, he began to have convulsions. The nurses and interns had placed him on a bed out in the center of the aisle between the beds in the ward; there they would have better access to the patient in their ministry. Ward C was a rather large ward and was full to overflowing. Actually, there was no other place for the patient's bed.

(Some time later I learned why I was called on that particular morning, for it puzzled me why a man whom I had never known

25

would send for me. In truth, the man did not himself send for me. One of the young doctors had sent for me immediately after the patient had recovered from the first spasm and asked for a minister.)

Rushing to the hospital in my car, I sprinted up the walkway to the elevator and hurried down the hallway to the west where Ward C was located. As I entered the room, I saw a sickening scene. The patient was going into convulsions again, and there were nurses and interns both at the head and foot of the bed endeavoring to restrain him. All the other patients in the ward were having their breakfast. The convulsive patient was lying fully exposed to all their views.

Immediately I said, "Don't you have any screens in this hospital to place around this patient so as to spare the other patients who are eating their breakfasts this awful scene?" The head nurse at once dispatched an orderly who brought screens, and we walled the patient off from the view of the rest of the patients in the ward.

As I moved up to the side of the bed, the patient became relaxed again and looked up into my face and said, "Will you read to me from God's word?"

Opening my New Testament, I began to read to him from John 14.

I had barely commenced to read when the patient said to me, "Will you go and call my father and mother—you go. They live in east Tennessee, and their number is . . . "

I ceased to read, went to a nearby telephone, and dialed the residence of the parents. They had already received word of the tragedy and said to me, "Tell him that we are getting ready now to leave, and we will be there at the very earliest!"

Returning to the bedside, I gave the patient the message from his parents and began to read again, "Let not your heart be troubled: believe in God, believe also in me. In my Father's house are many mansions; if it were not so, I would have told you; for I go to prepare a place for you. And if I go and prepare a place for you, I come again, and will receive you unto myself; that where I am, there ye may be also" (John 14:1-3, ASV).

Sensing the approach of another convulsion, I ceased to read. The patient looked up at me with a face of despair, saying, "Read on . . . for God's sake, don't stop!"

Again, I began to read from the promises of God, and for the second time the patient interrupted me, saying, "Please go and call my parents again, will you? Call them and tell them I said to hurry . . . please hurry!"

I went to the telephone and relayed the message to the parents, whereupon they gave me the same assurance that they were hastening and would arrive at the earliest possible moment.

On returning to the bedside of the patient, I began to speak to him about God's plan of salvation and how, if one is willing to do so, he is able to reverse his whole life-style—however short his days may be—if he will only put his faith in Christ Jesus. I told him the story of the thief on the cross who, in his dying moments, cried out to Jesus, by faith, and heard in response the life-giving words of Jesus as he said, "Today shalt thou be with me in Paradise" (Luke 23:43, ASV).

To those who do not know the ways of the Lord, it would be difficult, I know, to understand how God is able to save a sinner who has already arrived at the portals of death. But this is all God's work. It is not the work of human beings.

In the plan of salvation, the Heavenly Father lays down no timetable. Jesus did not say that if you would experience my saving grace, you must have at least ten years to live, or five years, or one year, or one month, or one day! He merely said, "For God so loved the world, that he gave his only begotten Son, that whosoever believeth on him should not perish, but have eternal life" (John 3:16, ASV).

By Christ's own words, then, we know that while there is life, there is hope, for it is by his mercy that he saves us. And we know that "As far as the east is from the west," (when we come to him by faith) "So far hath he removed our transgressions from us" (Ps. 103:12).

After my words concerning Jesus and the thief on the cross, a quiet calm seemed to pervade the whole frame of the man. Racked in pain as he had been, only moments before, he became as quiet and as peaceful as a babe in its mother's arms.

All the time he was looking up at me as I stood over him speaking. It seemed that he was afraid that he might lose a single word, and his keen, perceptive eyes were literally riveted on mine. He hardly seemed to bat an eye as he looked. Rather, he was straining with his eyes as though he were trying to see something clearly that had been so far off all the days of his life!

Carefully, I tried to prepare him for the inevitable. I told him, however, that God is able, always, to do far more than we ask or think.

I gave him assurance that if he would repent and take Christ as his Savior, his sins would be forgiven. Slowly, I spoke to him the words of hope and outlined for him, as best I could, the meaning of Jesus' words concerning repentance and faith as found in Mark 1:14-15.

After a few moments, I paused and said to him, "Do you understand clearly, now, what I have tried to say to you concerning God's plan of salvation?"

He said, "I think I do understand clearly."

Then resting his head on his pillow, with an upward look, and with the limbs of his body relaxed as they lay quietly under the white sheet, he said to me, "I do believe . . . I do . . . I do, and whether I live or whether I die, I will live or die trusting in Jesus! And I will follow him forever. I will never turn back."

Soon after he spoke those words, his body was tormented with pain again, and he went into another convulsion so intense that it required the strength of all us who were around his bed to restrain him—there were at least a half-dozen of us holding his hands, his arms, his feet, and his legs. I grasped his left hand at the wrist and his arm just above the elbow with both of my hands, while we all, together, held his body on the bed.

How long he lay in convulsion, I do not know, but it seemed to me for an age!

Finally, the pain-racked body began to relax, and the whole frame began to sink into a quiet, motionless stupor.

In another instant, the pallor of death began to spread over his face, and the eyes began to take on the look of death. The reflexes were all gone, and the respiration and the heartbeat! It was too late, now, for him to see his father and mother, but not for him to see God! For as he died, the rigid lines of agony left his face, leaving in their stead a soft, sweet smile of peace.

As I left Ward C and walked slowly toward the elevator and thence to my car, I thought again about the thief on the cross and about how wonderful it is that it is not by works of righteousness which we have done that God saves us but rather by the righteousness of God that comes to us through our faith!

It was not long afterward that the young doctor, then in residence at John Gaston, walked down the aisle of the First Baptist Church of Memphis asking for membership by baptism. I always felt that the experience we had together, along with the nurses and other doctors at John Gaston on that fateful morning, had made a lasting impact on his life even as it had on mine. We came to know, as never before, the exceeding greatness of the power of the Spirit's presence at the gate of death!

3

"I'm Goin' Home . . . I'm Not Goin'"

Henry Hope did not expect his days at The Southern Baptist Theological Seminary to be filled with flower-strewn pathways. No student looks for that when he is working his way through school with little, if any, financial support from home. Henry had been accustomed to making his way, and he was not afraid of work. He had always been industrious and ambitious.

Like many fledgling ministers of the gospel, he could have given up plans to attend the seminary upon his graduation from college, and many churches would have been happy to accept him without further training. For that matter, upon my own graduation from Wake Forest College, an invitation came to me to consider the pulpit of the First Baptist Church of Wilson, North Carolina. Flattered by the offer, I gladly went to preach on a given Sunday and to consider the pulpit.

The church received my message well, and the committee informed me that they were ready to recommend my name to the church for a call—if I would agree to accept a call as pastor. They informed me that a Wake Forest faculty member had recommended me for the position, and they were ready, after hearing me, to recommend that the church call me as pastor.

The committee even went so far as to suggest that I might be called with an understanding that if, after a tenure of two years, I felt the need of further theological training, they would give me a leave of absence for study. Happily, I did not need to wait two

30

years to feel the need of further training for the ministry. I felt the need right then.

What really woke me up to the need for further training was an incident that took place in the men's Bible class on the Sunday morning that I preached there. I was sitting with the group of men, quietly listening to the exposition of the teacher, and all at once, after dealing with a particularly involved theological matter, the teacher deferred to me for my views. Then and there, I realized that I was far from being ready to assume the pastorate of that church. Consequently, I went on to the seminary.

Henry Hope knew that he needed further training. He was willing to pay the price for it, and asked no special favors of anyone. Like many other students there, he went to the seminary on faith, believing that God would open a way for him to work and make the necessary money with which to pay for his books, his room, and his meals.

In those days, the student himself had no tuition to pay, for the tuition was taken care of by the Southern Baptist Convention's support of Southern Seminary. A student's expenses amounted, roughly, to his books, his board, and his room. The seminary asked for nothing more.

There were quite a number of opportunities at Southern Seminary then for a student to work his way. The vast acreage of "The Beeches" was covered in beautiful bluegrass that had to be mowed consistently during the spring, summer, and fall. The seminary buildings were kept warm by central heat that went out from a boiler room located near the central area of the campus. Coal had to be shoveled day and night, by hand, and the ashes and clinkers removed from the boiler daily. Classrooms had to be swept and tidied daily. Offices of professors had to be cared for. The seminary cafeteria also offered opportunities for student help. Henry Hope secured work in the boiler room of the seminary's heating plant. He fired the boiler at night, and this required the shoveling of tons and tons of coal.

One morning as I adjourned the class in Junior Greek, Henry Hope stood a few feet away waiting to speak to me. (At the death of Dr. A. T. Robertson, Dr. W. H. Davis, professor of Greek New Testament, had asked me to take charge of the class in Junior Greek for the remainder of the year while they sought a successor, for I was Dr. Robertson's student assistant.)

As my eye cut toward Hope, I noticed that he was neatly dressed, as though he had readied himself for a journey. When the class was adjourned, Hope approached me at the teacher's desk and said, quite nonchalantly, "I have just come to tell you good-bye."

"Good-bye!" I said. "What do you mean?"

"I am going home," he said. "I have broken my arm, and I can't hold my job any longer, and I am behind already with my room rent and other expenses; so I have to go." Then Henry Hope held up in my face the broken arm that had been dressed with splints and placed in a sling—as if to corroborate his words.

"Can you come by my office?" I said to him. "I know that it's only a short time until the chapel service, but I would like very much to see you alone, if you can come."

Hope followed me to Room 4 where I had my office as a student assistant, and I invited him to sit down and wait while I attended to two or three matters that were pressing.

Turning to Hope, I said, rather abruptly, "Why did you come to the seminary? Are you confident that you were called by God to be a preacher? Are you equally confident that you need further preparation, and that it was God's will for you to come to Southern Seminary to that end?"

Hope, seemingly frustrated at the kind of questions I was asking him in such Gatling-gunlike fashion, answered, "Of course I know that I need added preparation to be a preacher. Of course I am confident that I was called to preach and that God wanted me to come to this seminary to prepare myself for my task."

Interrupting him, I said, "Do you think that God's arm has

been shortened by the years? Do you believe that he is less powerful today than he was when he called you to preach? Do you really feel that if God wanted you to come to this seminary that he is not able to make a way for you to get along and to have your modest needs met in spite of a broken arm? What is a broken arm to God in the path of his mission, his calling?"

Henry Hope sat there for moments, as if in a daze. But the daze was a daze of astonishment, for I was opening up angles to his problem that he apparently had not even thought about.

Somehow I began to feel that there might be other factors in the decision to terminate his studies at the seminary for the year, and to Hope's surprise, I am sure, I said to him, "Is there any particular person back home that you are homesick to see, and could this be a factor in your decision to go home?"

Quite readily, he told me that his girlfriend was back home—the girl he hoped to marry one day—and that he just felt that he had to see her and talk over things with her. There was no intimation in his words, however, that he had anything to tell her but that he was terminating his studies for the year.

About this time, the chapel bell rang. Henry sat there as though expecting me to say, "Let us now go to chapel." Instead, I said, "You and I will not go to chapel today. We are going to have our own chapel service here in Room 4."

With those words, I turned to a passage in James that had been so helpful in my own life when I faced moments of indecision and began to read, "But if any of you lacketh wisdom, let him ask of God, who giveth to all liberally and upbraideth not; and it shall be given him. But let him ask in faith, nothing doubting: for he that doubteth is like the surge of the sea driven by the wind and tossed. For let not that man think that he shall receive anything of the Lord" (Jas. 1:5-7, ASV).

Then I turned and read another passage which has been to me a source of great strength and hope: "If ye abide in me, and my words abide in you, ask whatsoever ye will" (John 15:7, ASV).

Following the reading of the Scriptures, I invited Hope to kneel with me in prayer; but before the prayer began, I spoke at length with him about answered and unanswered prayer, trying to point out to him that the answer comes only to those who lean entirely on the leadership of Christ. There can be no room for ambivalence on the part of men of God. After all, the ambivalent man is an unstable man.

It has always been my conviction that a child of God is able to receive guidance from the Heavenly Father in dilemmas that he may face, if he will commit himself completely to following any course of action that God may outline for him. This is what Jesus was trying to say, as John records his words in 15:7. Abiding in Christ affects the whole life-style—every thought, every word, every deed. It is not a hop-and-skip matter, an off-and-on-again thing! One has to be committed, totally, to the will of God in his life in all situations. All personal bias must be done with! One has to say, in substance, "Lord, your way, your truth, and your life will be my life, my truth, my way; only reveal it to me, Lord, for that is all I ask!"

Now when a person can bring himself to that point, it is easy for him to receive guidance from the Lord, for the Lord will give him "the hunch," and he will know the way to go.

One has to be completely ready to receive the wisdom from God, the guidance, and he must have his mind already made up to follow that given course—just as a quarterback receives the football that is handed to him by the center. There can be no ambivalence at such a time—no equivocation.

When chapel adjourned, Henry Hope and I were still on our knees in prayer. First I had prayed earnestly for God to reveal to him his way, his will for him, and then I prayed for Hope to be able to perceive the will of God and to have the courage to seek to translate that will into action.

Following my prayer, Hope prayed a prayer such as I have rarely heard. His words fell from his lips as turbulent waters dash over a cataract. There was conviction in every word he uttered.

There was contrition, for he acknowledged that he had been in a state of doubt, and distrust, whereas he was supposed to be a man of faith. He acknowledged his sin and begged forgiveness. His words rolled on as though he were one trying to convince the Lord of his sincerity, and of the depth of his faith, and of his desire to trust his providing care, come what might!

After Hope closed his prayer, I prayed again, and then closed my own prayer and slowly rose to my feet. Hope, sensing that I was standing, arose to his feet, and these words, spoken with great feeling, fell from his lips, "I'm stayin'! I'm not goin'!"

Hope's cheeks were bathed with tears. I knew that I was standing face-to-face now with a man of purpose, a man of faith. I could see courage written all over his countenance and something of the unflinchable resolve that Tennyson visualized in the faces of the men in "The Charge of the Light Brigade."

The following Monday, Henry Hope came back to my office again, but on a totally different mission. On this occasion he had no problem to solve, no need to be met! He merely came to share with me a great blessing that had come to him over the weekend.

Speaking excitedly, he said, "You know something wonderful happened this morning. The mail brought me a check that cares for my every need. I can now pay up my room rent. I now have money for food. I can pay my doctor's bill. And I can wait for my arm to get good and strong before I go back to work. Isn't God wonderful?"

At the end of that seminary year, as Henry Hope and I chanced to meet in the rotunda of Norton Hall, he drew me aside and said, "I just want a word or two with you before I leave for home." With a twinkle in his eye, he said, "I am *really going* this time, but before I go, I want to thank you for what you did for me that day when you counseled with me and prayed with me in Room 4."

"It was not I, Henry," I said, "who did this wonderful thing for you. It was the Lord. It was not I who convinced you that you ought to remain at the seminary, notwithstanding your predicament. It was the Holy Spirit that came and took charge of your life as you yielded your life to him fully."

Actually I had had a personal experience somewhat analogous to that of Henry Hope, but also widely different in its character. There was a time during my seminary days that I was literally "broke," so far as funds were concerned. This was occasioned by the fact that the country church I was serving had gotten behind with my salary.

One day I felt that I had literally come to a dead end. I had no thought, of course, about leaving the seminary and terminating my training, but I did not know which way to turn.

Shortly before the noon hour, I said to my beloved wife, "I am going over to the church for a while; I do not know what time I will be back; just don't expect me for lunch today!" Fern asked no questions because she knew that I was troubled, and she observed that I had in my hand the little brown, much-worn leather folder in which I kept all matters relating to finances. She was thoroughly aware of the problem.

Going into the church sanctuary, I sat down at the Lord's Supper table and spread out all of my bills before me, and the record of my expenditures over the past month. The bills were not large ones—even for that day. One could go to a grocery store then and get a whole supply of groceries for $3 to $4—two large bags of groceries!

But my bills needed to be paid and I had no money. I knew only that if the church would pay me the salary due, according to the promise, everything would be all right.

Finally, with the papers spread out all over the table, I got down on my knees and began to pray earnestly for the Heavenly Father to show me the way. Like a little child, I held up my hands to him in desperation, but yet in perfect faith.

Finally a quiet peace filled my heart, and my mind was at rest. And well might it have been at rest, for on the following Monday morning, the little church I was serving (wholly without any knowledge of my problem, and without any word from me) paid up all of my back salary. I could have shouted when the treasurer handed me the check, face up, and I saw the amount. Every dollar the church owed me was included in the check.

Like Henry Hope, I had an experience, all my own, that I will never forget. The Holy Spirit also came to me with loving assurance in my hour of need!

4

Dr. Will Brown

Late on a weekday afternoon, the phone rang in my office at the First Baptist Church of Memphis, Tennessee. (The church was then at the old location at Linden and Lauderdale.) The voice on the other end of the line, firm and strong, said, "This is Dr. Will Brown. I'd like to come and see you if you will tell me when to do so."

We still had streetcars in Memphis, though a number of city buses had begun to operate, and Dr. Will explained that he would have to come by streetcar. The appointment for the conference was set, and he walked slowly into my office at the appointed hour, right to the minute.

The moment Dr. Will entered the office, I was greatly impressed by him. He was a tall man of sturdy build, and with a strong, ruddy face like that of a patriarch. He had hardly more than sat down when he said to me, "I have come to ask you if you will conduct my funeral, when the time comes. I have everything else taken care of and, I think, in good order. But I do not have anyone to conduct my funeral. Will you do it?"

I told him there was a possibility that I might be the first one "to go," but that if I were around at the time of his decease, I would certainly be available to officiate at his funeral service should the family desire me to do so.

Then I switched the subject to what I regarded to be a more relevant theme, saying, "Dr. Will, now I have a question to ask you . . . a question which I regard to be far more important than the one you have just asked me, and which I have sought to answer." Dr. Will seemed stunned for a moment by my remark, but with a twinkle in his eye said, "Go ahead; ask it!"

In a quiet, gentle way I told him that if I were to conduct his funeral service there was one thing I would like to know about in advance and that was his relationship to the Savior. Then looking directly at him I said, "Do you know Jesus? Have you committed your life to him as Savior and Lord? Have you followed him in baptism and church membership?"

To all of these questions, Dr. Will gave a negative answer, saying, "I have thought about these matters, but I have never taken any positive step."

Then I began to talk to him at length about the importance of coming to know Jesus and of the significance of total commitment of one's life to him as "the way, the truth, and the life." All the while he listened with rapt attention to every word I said, giving me in return no word of dissent. I could tell that he was deeply moved by my words and that the seed I had planted had fallen in good soil!

Allowing the subject to rest for a few moments, I said to him, "Tell me about yourself, Dr. Will. When did you come to Memphis, and from where did you come? Where were you born?"

Responding with great animation to my questions, he began to tell me about his forebears, of the farm on which he lived as a boy in east Tennessee, and of some of his experiences. He found in me a ready audience, for I felt that there was in store for me some interesting dialogue.

Dr. Will began by saying, "I came from east Tennessee. My forebears settled there on a land grant from the king of England, and some of the family still remain in the area."

Jumping about in his conversation, as he recalled the days of his childhood, he said, "I was a very forceful character when I was young. I had a good, rugged physique, and I used it no little!" Then he added, as if to justify that statement, "I engaged in no few fights. In fact, I was ready to take on any person that came my way and crossed me in the least measure."

Then he told me a story that threw me into spasms of laughter. He said, "One day a young dandy came our way in the community, and it just seemed to me he felt too wise and too important. In fact, he began to talk about his physical strength and how he had always been able to take on anyone who came his way.

"After listening to about all I could stand of the young man's remarks, I spoke up. This seemed to irritate him to the point that he said something back to me at which I took sharp offense. Immediately I waded into him with my fists, but I can only remember one swing at him.

"Evidently the fellow took the next swing at me, for he knocked me completely out and left me lying on the ground as cold as a turnip pulled fresh from the ground on a frosty morning. When I awoke, he was nowhere to be seen—he had gone!"

Dr. Will then told me another story: "I tell you when I was young, I was tough . . . tough as a pine knot! They just didn't come any tougher than I was!

"One day a mad dog came through our community. The dog bit a neighbor's cow, and the cow died. The dog bit a neighbor's dog, and the dog died. The dog bit a neighbor's mule, and the mule died."

And he added, "Then the dog bit me, and the dog died!"

Feeling that it was time to turn the conversation back to the main subject, I pressed Dr. Will for a response incident to his willingness to receive Jesus as Savior and Lord. Immediately I saw that I had moved too fast with my persuasion, for he replied, "I'll just have to think about that. You give me time and let me think it over. That's quite a step you are suggesting that I take at this stage in my life!"

Soon thereafter Dr. Will indicated that it was time for him to "go now" but that he would be back to see me again within the next day or so. We then had prayer together, and he went out.

A few days later, Dr. Will called for another appointment, and again he was there in my office right on schedule.

As soon as he had sat down, he said to me, "If I will agree to what you have asked, will you baptize me privately?"

Replying, I said, "Dr. Will, we Baptists may do a lot of things in a corner, but baptism is not one of them. I cannot give you private baptism for the simple reason that to me and to many others who are of the Baptist persuasion the ordinance would have lost its true meaning.

"Baptism," I explained to him, "as we Baptists hold it, is not a means of salvation; rather, it is only a symbol of vital truth and that without saving efficacy.

"Baptism is a testimonial," I said, "a form of witness whereby the one being baptized declares to the world, 'By this act I testify to the fact that I am a follower of Jesus and that I believe in the resurrection of the dead. I believe that Jesus arose from the grave on the third day just as he promised his troubled disciples, and I believe that I will rise from the dead on the day of his return, when I will be with him and in his presence forever! I believe also that in coming to follow Jesus I begin a new life-style, and by this baptism I symbolize the death of my old life-style. In going down into the water I portray the burial of all my past. In coming up out of the water, I testify to my belief in my own resurrection here and now, while in the flesh, and at the last day, and to a new way of life—the Jesus way.' "

Dr. Will listened intently throughout my discussion of baptism. Then, pensively, he looked out of the window toward the south, pondering my words for some moments, after which he turned and said to me in a crisp, clear voice, "I will do it; you can baptize me before all the people, if you want to, for from now on I will try to be a follower of Jesus."

The baptism of Dr. Will Brown, who had practiced dentistry in Memphis down in his old office on South Second Street for more than fifty years, took place on schedule. But it was no ordinary baptism. I did not dream, nor did anyone else (I am sure) contemplate, the dimensions of the transformation that had taken place in his life.

Why it is true, I will never know, but always when a man advanced in years goes down into the waters of baptism, it seems to be regarded as an unusual triumph for Christianity. To see a man of wisdom, a man of years, capitulate to Christ and start all over again, and especially at the advanced age of an octogenarian, has always been for many people a thing of unusual romance.

Personally, I have never been able to see it quite that way. To me the greatest romance in baptism is that of leading down into the baptismal waters a young person who, with great understanding and with solid resolve and total commitment, decides to become a follower of Jesus Christ for all the future days. I think of the possibilities of such a life invested in the cause of Christ at such a young and tender age.

Seldom does one who becomes a follower of Christ so late in life accomplish, in the eyes of the world, much for the eyes of people to see. But this was not to be the case of Dr. Will Brown. No one dreamed of what was to take place in his life, henceforth, as he came up out of the baptismal waters.

Though Dr. Will was not too steady on his feet, he stood as straight as a ramrod, in walking, and had the bearing of one who had spent his life in the military. No top sergeant, barking out his orders to his men, could have stood more erect than Dr. Will as he stood there in the baptismal waters awaiting baptism!

Immediately after his baptism, Dr. Will seemed to be overwhelmed with a desire to make up for lost time in his relationship to Jesus. First he asked me if he might have a calling card printed, bearing the name of the church and my name as pastor, and then, in the lower left-hand corner, his own name. He said, "I want these to pass out on the bus and the streetcar as I go to and from my office." He had the cards printed, and the print job was in exceeding good taste.

Very soon, on a Sunday morning, at the singing of the invitation hymn, I saw Dr. Will move out of a pew two-thirds of the way back in the sanctuary holding the left arm of a sailor from the nearby Millington naval base and walk side by side with him down the aisle. As I reached out my hand to grasp his hand and then that of the young man, he said to me, "Here is a young man who wants to become a follower of Jesus."

This kind of event involving Dr. Will took place again and again at the worship services in the days immediately following.

One day when he was in my office, I said to him, "Dr. Will, tell me how you go about your approach to a lost soul. How do you make your beginning? What do you say?"

Dr. Will replied, "Well, most of my contacts take place as I go and come from work. As I enter the streetcar or bus," he said, "I try to pick out a prospect—one to whom I think I can witness. Then I will politely ask if I may sit by him. After we have ridden a little way, if my seat partner is a man, I may take hold of the lapel of his coat and say to him, 'My, but that's a beautiful suit you have on; where did you get it? I might want to get one myself.'" He explained he went from there to the more important matter of talking with the man about his soul.

How many individuals Dr. Will Brown witnessed to and brought into the First Baptist Church of Memphis, I do not know. I wish I had kept account of them, but I failed to do so. Once I tried to estimate, not long before he died, how many people I had baptized as a result of his witness. I estimated then that there were about forty.

Once I watched him as he walked down the aisle holding the arm of a newfound friend whom he was bringing to make his confession as a follower of Jesus, and I noticed how frail he was, and literally how "wobbly" his legs were. Later I said to him, "Dr. Will, for one as far advanced in years as you are, it is so natural for one to use a cane; why don't you do so? I believe you would walk with a sense of greater security."

To my question he curtly replied, but with the same twinkle in his eye, "You want to know why I do not use a cane? I will tell you: I am too proud!"

Well do I recall looking out over the great congregation of the First Baptist Church of Memphis, again and again, on Sunday morning, or at the Sunday evening worship service, and seeing a number of individuals to whom Dr. Will had witnessed and brought to Jesus. He reminded me, in his efforts to win the lost, of Andrew, who found "his own brother," saying to him, "We have found the Messiah," and then "brought him unto Jesus" (John 1:41-42, ASV).

Few churches in our land are likely to see the like of Dr. Will Brown—a man who at eighty-two years of age became a convinced believer and a dedicated soul-winner, always on the quest for the lost.

What was the secret of this unforgettable character, this extraordinary man, who in the years of the sharp decline of his physical health became a stirring challenge to youth and age to follow Jesus?

So far as I am concerned, there is only one answer to this phenomenon: the Holy Spirit! I saw this man struggle with the old life-style as the challenge of Jesus was presented to him in a direct, uncompromising manner. I saw him sit without wincing, listening raptly to every word as though he were drinking a potion which he knew he needed—a potion which might, at the moment, have had for him an overtone of bitterness—for he was being challenged to change his whole way of life in favor of a life-style that was radically different from anything of which he had ever dreamed!

As he sat in my study that day, at the moment of decision, I felt a strange awareness of a Presence that was beyond our own. I saw him yield to the convincing, convicting power of the Holy Spirit and pass from darkness unto light . . . from death unto life! And I knew that this mighty transformation was no work of mine. In a way, I was only a bystander. The Holy Spirit accomplished the mighty work of God's grace.

And now I understood better the words of Jesus, saying, "Nevertheless I tell you the truth: It is expedient for you that I go away; for if I go not away, the Comforter will not come unto you; but if I go, I will send him unto you. And he, when he is come, will convict the world in respect of sin, and of righteousness, and of judgment" (John 16:7-8, ASV).

5

Tornadoes in Texas

What does the Holy Spirit have to do with tornadoes? Much, you might say, if you should ever have the experience that was mine on my first commercial airplane flight long years ago. Up until that time, I had had one flight in a plane—a very small, one-engine craft with room for only one passenger. I remember climbing into that plane on a rainy night and sitting down beside the veteran pilot, Mr. Bothwell Lee of Augusta, Georgia. The door to the cabin, when I closed it, banged like the door of my father's old T-Model Ford that I used to drive in 1917.

My first flight on a commercial airplane began early one afternoon when my wife drove me to what later was to become Daniel Field in Augusta for my flight to San Antonio, Texas. I had a speaking engagement there the next day.

The weather was lovely in Augusta that afternoon, and we had almost a cloudless sky. I remarked to Fern that it was going to be a beautiful day for the flight, but what I did not know then was that beyond the horizon already a storm was brewing—a storm coughing up a whole string of tornadoes that would play hop and skip directly in our flight path.

One cannot tell much about the weather ahead as he climbs aboard a plane for a flight, whatever the direction. For one thing, one can only see ahead approximately fourteen miles, at the ground level, because the curvature of the earth's surface obscures a farther view. On that day, however, without such reckoning, I merely assumed that it was going to be a beautiful flight . . . all the way!

As I stood to board the plane, a fellow passenger from New York was standing near, and I remarked to him, "That's a beautiful plane, isn't it?"

In a rather disconsolate manner, he replied, "Oh, I suppose so, if a thing that is bright and shiny is beautiful!" The plane was a two-motor affair—either a DC-3 or a Dakota, I do not remember which.

As we flew along on our journey, we began to encounter dark clouds to the west of us—clouds that spread all the way from the south to the north. A cool front that lay directly ahead of us was moving eastward—right into our face—but I didn't give a thought to tornadoes!

Although I had read about them and had seen pictures of them, I knew little about tornadoes. We seldom have more than a semblance of them in the mountains where I grew up!

As we approached Jackson, Mississippi, where we were supposed to make our first stop, the pilot calmly announced that because of the low ceiling we would continue westward without a stop at Jackson. He said we might stop at Little Rock, Arkansas, or some other nearby point across the Mississippi River. However, we did not stop at Little Rock, for the winds of the approaching storm, and the rain, had become far more severe by then.

As we made our way westward toward Dallas, the winds became more and more violent and the turbulence severe. Still, we made a good landing at Dallas. After refueling, and a reasonable period of waiting for the storm to subside, the announcement came over the loudspeaker that our flight would proceed westward. The announcer assured us that the worst of the storm, so far as our flight was concerned, should be over.

Being somewhat wary of the weather ahead, after what we had already encountered, and being an inexperienced flier, I was hesitant to board the plane with the other passengers.

As always, in such moments of indecision, I decided to pray about the matter and seek guidance from the Lord.

Finding a deserted corridor in the terminal, I knelt for prayer, claiming God's promise found in James which says, "But if any of you lacketh wisdom, let him ask of God, who giveth to all liberally and upbraideth not; and it shall be given him. But let him ask in faith, nothing doubting: for he that doubteth is like the surge of the sea driven by the wind and tossed. For let not that man think that he shall receive anything of the Lord; a doubleminded man, unstable in all his ways" (Jas. 1:5-8, ASV). I remember saying, "Lord, this is your mission—I am going for you; tell me if I should go on! You know how I feel, Lord; but I know that if it is thy will for me to make this engagement, you will see me through!"

Along with the rest of the passengers, I climbed aboard; for I felt that I had received the "hunch" from God to go ahead. I felt that I was moving in the circle of his will and that all would be well in the end.

Little did I surmise, as I climbed aboard the plane that evening, that I was to have the experience of a lifetime, so far as tornadoes were concerned. Since then I have been in flights where tornadoes were involved, but I never experienced anything like I did on that occasion.

As we sped along from Dallas, it soon became obvious that we had not left the tornado belt, nor were the tornadoes leaving us! It appeared rather that we were going to have a face-to-face encounter with a tornado.

It was now nighttime, and I could not see a single star as I peered out of the window on the starboard side of the plane. Every view from the window was that of dark, threatening clouds which were everywhere. Now and then the darkness was partially dispelled, for an instant, by keen flashes of lightning that lit up the whole sky.

Presently the plane began to dash, and lunge, and all but roll like craft of the old barnstormers of a generation ago.

It was an eerie feeling, I must confess, for at times the plane would surge upward like a seagull with its wings spread in the face of strong wind over the sea. Then, like a pelican that darts downward with folded wings, its feet tucked close to its body for a dive into the sea for a fish, the plane seemed to go downward. Then it would surge upward again, and then downward—and up and down, and up and down!

Finally, as we continued to pitch and toss on the flight to San Antonio, the stewardess, beginning at the front cabin window, closed the curtains on each side of the craft so the passengers would not be able to see the electrical display of the storm. I was seated in the rear of the plane, on the right side, and in the last seat.

After the stewardess had closed my curtains and was returning to the front part of the cabin, I decided to open my curtains, reckoning, "After all, I am a paying passenger; if I want to see this display of lightning, that should be my privilege!"

Upon opening the curtain, I looked out upon what I am sure was the most brilliant display of lightning that I shall ever see. It was almost as spectacular as some of the fireworks displays that one sees at the county fair or at some of the jubilee celebrations observed in large cities. I took out my watch and counted exactly 120 flashes of lightning to the minute—that's two each second! A solid sheet of water plunged off the rear edge of the plane's wing.

Finally I closed the curtain, and when I had done so, I tightened my seat belt more tightly, for I must confess I had deep feelings of apprehension. After all, the plane was being dashed about almost as a piece of paper is swept about with a strong wind.

Opening my Greek New Testament at the fourteenth chapter of John, I began to read the words of Jesus: "Let not your heart be troubled: believe in God, believe also in me" (14:1, ASV). And I remembered how Dr. A. T. Robertson of Southern Seminary had once translated the passage, "Let not your hearts flutter; you believe in God, believe also in me." Then I read

Jesus' words which John records later on in the chapter, "Peace I leave with you; my peace I give unto you. . . . Let not your heart be troubled, neither let it be fearful."

Having read this, I closed the New Testament, leaned back in my seat, and thought of the prayer in the airport, and of the words of Jesus which I had just read. Then there fell audibly from my lips the unrehearsed words of assurance that I have thought of scores of times in the years that have followed: "My Pilot knows the storms!"

For he was there, in the storm he made, directing its every moment, and I was conscious of his Presence and of the mission on which he had sent me. And his Presence banished my fears.

6

Hope for the Alcoholic

It was late in the morning, and I had just arrived at my office at the First Baptist Church of Memphis. My secretary said, "You have a very urgent call from a family, and they want you to come to their apartment immediately if you can do so." I asked for the address, and when I found that it was in a ghettolike part of the city, I suspected that the problem might have to do with beverage alcohol, for only recently I had been called to another home in that area with such a problem.

The problem of beverage alcohol is a very ancient one. It was very definitely a problem in the days of the children of Israel, for the ancient wise men warned the people saying, "Wine is a mocker, strong drink a brawler; And whosoever erreth thereby is not wise" (Prov. 20:1, ASV). "Woe unto them that rise up early in the morning," said the prophet Isaiah, "that they may follow strong drink; that tarry late into the night, till wine inflame them!" (5:11). And the apostle Paul said in his first epistle to the Corinthians, "Know ye not that the unrighteous shall not inherit the kingdom of God? Be not deceived: neither fornicators, nor idolaters, nor adulterers, nor effeminate, nor abusers of themselves with men, nor thieves, nor covetous, nor drunkards, nor revilers, nor extortioners shall inherit the kingdom of God" (6:9-10, ASV).

The first acquaintance I had with beverage alcohol was as a lad when I was in the sixth grade of the local elementary school. Up until that time I knew nothing about its effects on the human body. There was never any of it in our home—neither wine, beer, nor liquor, and I had never seen any of my friends drink before.

But late in the afternoon of a hot summer day, when I had gone to the country store for my mother to purchase some articles that she needed, one of my classmates, Jim Doolittle, came up just as I was leaving the store. He was all but dead drunk! He was on his feet, and walking—after a fashion; but at times he reeled almost as a boxer who had received a right hook to the jaw from the burly fist of Muhammad Ali.

I had never before seen a drunk person. I knew, of course, the story about Jim's father. He was a medical doctor, and I always heard it said he had had a brilliant mind. But he became a victim of beverage alcohol and died in his early thirties. Everyone lamented his death because it took away from the community the only practicing physician.

Seeing my schoolmate friend, Jim Doolittle, under the effects of alcohol was enough to fix my mind against the use of it forever. Of course, I had been taught in the home to abstain from the use of liquor, and I had seen the printed covenant of the Baptist church which I attended and was aware that it pledged us to "abstain" from both the use and the sale of intoxicating beverages.

One of the things that troubled me about the liquor problem was the saying that little could be done to help a person who became an addict. Many people seemed to just "write him off" as one without promise and without hope. I suppose there was felt to be some basis for this premise, for the apostle Paul in his letter to the Ephesians said, "Therefore do not be foolish, but understand what the will of the Lord is. And do not get drunk with wine, for that is debauchery" (5:17-18, RSV).

A careful examination of the word which Paul used and which is translated "debauchery" in the Revised Standard Version reveals a far deeper meaning than that. The word Paul used is the ancient Greek word *asotia*. This word is the one used to mark the character of an *asotos* man, that is, an abandoned man—a hopeless man. A man in a drunken state cannot be saved *while he is in that state*. This is true for the simple reason that while one is in a drunken state, he is not in position to reason and to make a choice concerning the destiny of his life. He is incapable of opening the door of his heart and letting the cleansing Spirit of Christ enter so as to effect reconciliation with God. Such a person is both helpless, and hopeless, while he is in that state.

But the Bible tells us that there is hope for the alcoholic.

In the passage we quoted from Paul's Corinthian letter, we quoted only verses 9 and 10 which present the bold affirmation that adulterers, homosexuals, idolaters, thieves, drunkards, and other immoral people cannot inherit the kingdom of God.

But this is what Paul went on to say in verse 11: "And such were some of you: but ye were washed, but ye were sanctified, but ye were justified in the name of the Lord Jesus Christ, and in the Spirit of our God" (1 Cor. 6:11, ASV).

Herein lies the hope for the alcoholic. The alcoholic, just as a thief, just as an adulterer, just as the greedy, just as the robber, can be "washed," as the old hymn writers put it, "in the blood of the lamb." They used to sing that old hymn in the Traphill Baptist Church when I was a small boy. I could not understand the song at first. Then when I came to grasp the fact that the hymn writer was only speaking symbolically of the meaning of the shedding of Christ's blood on the cross for all who would turn to him by faith, the words came to have meaning for me. In the ear of memory, I can hear the little group of believers now as they sang: "Are you washed in the blood,/In the soul-cleansing blood of the Lamb?"

After all, had not John said as he looked upon Jesus, "Behold, the Lamb of God, that taketh away the sin of the world!" (John 1:29, ASV)? And Peter graphically portrayed his concept of the cleansing power of the blood of Christ in his first epistle, saying, "Who his own self bare our sins in his body upon the tree, that we, having died unto sins, might live unto righteousness; by whose *blood-trickling wounds* ye were healed. For ye were going astray like sheep; but are now returned unto the Shepherd and Bishop of your souls" (1 Pet. 2:24-25, AT).

Again and again in my ministry, I have seen the alcoholic turn to God and be completely delivered—as we used to say in the mountains—"lock, stock, and barrel!" I could document case after case of those whose lives have been thus transformed as they came under the cleansing, healing power of the Holy Spirit. The examples are many, but I will only share one with you at this time.

Upon reaching the address my secretary had given me, I climbed an ill-kept stairway and entered the apartment of the family who had called for me. There I found myself in a situation such as I had never experienced before. Both the husband and the wife were dyed-in-the-wool alcoholics, and had just re-covered from a drunken state. They were now completely rational and knew that they had reached, at long last, what the Frenchman would call the cul-de-sac—the dead end. They had come to realize, as they sat and talked together that morning, that they simply had to change their way of life. They recognized that they could not go on in their old life-style any longer.

As I stood and looked about, I realized that I had never before been in an apartment quite so unkept, so drab, so unlovely, and so poor. I had been into scores of poor homes, but I had never seen one that looked like this one.

There were two rooms with few furnishings. The plastered walls were marked with wide, gaping holes. Some of the plaster had fallen from the ceiling, leaving the latticework exposed. Everything was dirty, unkempt, and bore the marks of poverty at its worst.

There was an old trunk against the wall in the south side of the living room, and I finally sat down on it to talk.

The children had gone to school—children lovely to look upon, I later found as I saw them face-to-face, children with real promise.

As soon as I sat down, the wife, speaking for herself and her husband, said, "We have called you to help us, for we know that we can't go on like this any longer. We have reached the end of our rope! Alcohol has wrecked us, and we want you to tell us if there is any hope. Can you show us the way out of this awful situation?"

Speaking freely, and seemingly with understanding, she continued, "We know you have had a lot of experience with people like us, and we know that you have been able to help many of them, for we have heard of your work. We are ready and willing to do anything on earth that you ask us to do, if you will only help us! Please help us!"

Beginning with verses from the Scriptures which I quoted freely, I began to show them how God had brought them to a wonderful moment in their lives, a moment when they had understanding concerning their problem, and that he had also given them a desire to do something about it.

This is basically the point in life that an alcoholic must reach if he is to receive help and conquer his habit. He must come to understand the necessity for a complete change in his life-style, and he must desire to make that change.

When a person comes to this point and willingly and earnestly turns to the Lord for salvation, wisdom, and guidance, and has the assistance of a Christian counselor who has had experience in counseling with those afflicted with such problems, Satan and all of his angels cannot thwart the miracle of change that is bound to come.

All through the conversation, the couple sat with strained attention, speaking only when I would ask them a question, and hungering to receive, it seemed, every word that I uttered. I almost felt that I could see their true selves leaning out from their disordered, dispirited bodies and holding out to me their unseen hands of their spirits as if to say, "Please take our hands and lead us, and help us . . . please . . . please . . . please!"

Reading to them at length from the Scriptures, I explained to them how it was necessary for the Spirit of God to cleanse them and to enter their lives with wisdom and power if they were to begin effectively, and forever continue, the new life-style that is in Christ.

I was amazed at the perception that their words revealed. They seemed to understand every word I spoke. It was not as though I were speaking to them in a language of an unknown tongue, but rather, they seemed to drink in every word with understanding. Now I know, as I did not realize at the moment, that it was the Holy Spirit that had come into our midst and was hovering over us all and filling their minds with conviction and understanding. Already they were convicted of sin, but now they were becoming convicted of righteousness, and of the judgment!

And there, in the hallowed quiet of that late morning hour, and after a long season of counseling, I saw them pass the great divide—the divide that separates the lost from the saved . . . the divide that separates the old life-style from the new life-style that is in Christ.

As we arose from the knees of prayer and commitment, I looked into their eyes, reddened both by the inebriate state from which they had recently emerged, and the emotional trauma through which they were passing in turning loose of the old life. I felt that here was a conversion experience that was genuine— and a viable reaching out for the new way that is in Christ Jesus.

Here were two people who had really been saved, that very moment! I was confident that they had been delivered from the power of strong drink and that the past would soon become only a memory.

And that is exactly what took place. On the following Sunday, both the husband and wife professed their faith in Christ and were baptized. And I can recall, to this moment, the look of radiant hope which I saw in their eyes as they emerged from the baptismal waters.

One by one, the children became Christ's followers and united with the church, as they came to the age of reason.

Tragically, the husband was only to enjoy his newfound joys for little more than one year, for after a few months had passed, the hand of an incurable disease lay hold of him and took him away in death.

But Lem Rhodes died a saved man. Not once did he return to strong drink. Not once did he break his vow.

Not once did his wife Rose break her vow—nor has she till this day. She lives with her oldest daughter who has been a model of Christian womanhood in the years that have followed. And recently I received a beautiful letter from the mother and the daughter—a letter that bore witness to the same triumphant faith and hope and love in Christ Jesus that marked them on the day in which they put on Christ and his way.

Hope for the alcoholic? Of course there is hope! There is hope for all people in every sin situation, no matter how far down in the vortex of human profligacy and shame they have been sucked in by the engulfing waves of circumstance, if they will only turn to Christ by faith and yield their lives to the empowering, guiding presence of the Holy Spirit and the blessed hope of his redeeming love.

7

Mending a Broken Vessel

It had been a long, hard year at the Southern Baptist seminary where I had enrolled three years before. Like all the students there, when the last day of the spring classes was over, I began to look forward to the vacation that lay ahead. The brightest part of the vacation was a trip to the home of my beloved parents in western North Carolina. I had always loved the Blue Ridge Mountains. I was born there, and the earliest view I remember was looking out upon the mountain we called "Greenstreets," just to the west of our home near Traphill in Wilkes County.

But this year the longing for a change was even more intense. Some months before, I had been called to serve as pastor of the Grace Baptist Church of Redbud, Kentucky—a small band of believers who had separated themselves from the mother church, the Covenant Baptist of Redbud, and formed a new congregation.

When I was called to become the pastor of the church, I understood that it was a fragmented body, but I had no idea of what lay before me, and what the future held for us all.

The community of Redbud lay at the heart of beautiful Lake County, Kentucky—a county that was noted for its spacious fields of blue grass, and for the hardy race of men and women who made their living from the soil. The county as a whole was rural. Laketon, the county seat, with well-kept homes and gardens, the red brick courthouse, and the jail, had a main street with clusters of small shops where people came for their weekly trading from all over the county.

The village of Redbud was much smaller. In the village was a bank (which failed like many other banks in the Great Depression), a post office, two groceries, a garage, the churches, and many picturesque homes which lined the road on either side as the road was indeed the center of the town.

The whole countryside was lovely. In the spring there was redbud everywhere, and you felt, at times, as if the bushes (almost trees) had been planted so as to elicit the greatest aesthetic appeal.

The very contour of the earth was beautiful. Some of the hills (knobs, they were sometimes called) looked as if they had been carefully shaped by human hands. These knobs and their slopes, and the rolling fields of grass that spread out in every direction, were surpassingly beautiful, whether in spring or in autumn.

Along the banks of the streams one could see the shelflike patterns of limestone rock that lay beneath the deep soil that nurtured blue grass. The arresting forms of light and shadow, as the late sun fell upon the craggy banks, were exhilarating to the eye.

The Covenant Church was an old and well-established church—the very hub of the religious life of the community. In it were the descendants of hardy pioneers—sturdy men and women who were solid and upright in their ways, impeccably moral. By farming, raising cattle, and dairying, they earned their livelihood.

There was one doctor in the Redbud Community, Dr. Richard Lee, who had practiced medicine for more than a half century. He had taught a Bible class in the Covenant Church for many years, and his wife, Ruby, had also taught.

The people of the Redbud Community, with few exceptions, were churchgoing people. For generations they had gone together, many of them walking side by side, to the Covenant

Church. Through their loving gifts, and with their own strong hands, they had built a lovely edifice—small, but adequate for that day. Even a casual glance at the church, from within and without, made it obvious to the onlooker that here was a people who loved their church house and who frequented it at the hours of worship.

In church, the families married off their young. There they brought their babies soon after their birth, with the family at hours of worship. From within their sacred walls they went out to bury their dead.

The church cemetery lay to the southwest and not far away. There, for generations, they had laid to rest the bodies of their beloved dead.

It was a peace-loving community, and one in which there was perennial sharing with one another in times of sorrow or distress. Lovingly they kept vigil during the long hours of night when a loved one lay ill and near death. And when death came, the love they shared with one another brought comfort.

Great quantities of food would be brought in by loving neighbors during the crisis—enough food not only for the immediate family but for family and friends from afar as they would come to share in the time of sorrow. Flowers were sent, and letters were written. Gentle hands of loving care took over the home and performed the chores of the home until the crisis was over.

But something terrible happened in the Covenant Church one day. Just how it happened, and just what brought it on, I never knew—nor did I want to know. Already I knew enough, as the young pastor who had come to lead the "splinter" group. I knew that something terrible had driven people apart, had fragmented the mother congregation, and had split whole families—leaving brother against brother, sister against sister, and friend against friend.

The people did not discuss what had taken place. They

remained inflexibly tight-lipped about it all. I never once asked a question, for such a question would have been far too personal. The roots of the problem went deep. And like the roots of the ancient papyrus plant in the marshy waters of the Nile, they stretched out in every direction. I suppose the condition might be described as a sort of spiritual malaise that rested, like the somber clouds of a dark, unseasonable winter, over all the countryside— a malaise that marked not merely the onset of a spiritual disease that afflicted every household, but a condition that grew worse day by day.

The splinter church, called "Grace Baptist," met in a small one-story building that once housed a store on the western edge of the village. It had been carefully refurbished and converted into a very respectable meeting place for the small band of believers (about seventy-one). The members were dutiful in their attendance at all the gatherings, and loving and kind in their concern for the young pastor.

At hog-killing time the members would share generous amounts of their delectable sausage which was preserved in long, cloth, cylinder-shaped bags for the winter. They were lavish in their gifts of country produce, home-canned goods, butter, and milk. I often thought how much more difficult, economically, the days at the seminary might have been during one particular winter had it not been for the love gifts from the church.

When I was called to supply at the church, I was serving as pastor of the Knobs Baptist Church, situated near the town of Lance, Kentucky. Although my work at the Knobs Church had proved to be a rewarding experience from the beginning, somehow I felt led of the Lord to consider the invitation to preach at the Grace Church.

At that time I knew nothing whatever about the Grace Church; I knew only that they wanted a "trial sermon." After thinking over the invitation, I called the chairman of the pulpit committee and asked if they were considering anyone else for the pastorate.

When they assured me that no one else was before the church as a prospective pastor, I told them I would come and preach for them on the appointed Sunday.

On my first visit to the church, it was a case of "love at first sight." I fell in love with the people, and apparently they had a deep regard for me—enough so that they immediately proposed to call me as their pastor, if I would give them any assurance of my acceptance. I finally came to the conclusion that if the church should call me unanimously, without a single dissenting vote, that God was leading me to the work. The call was extended, and there was no dissenting vote.

I was aware, of course, that the church was a splinter group, and this gave me great hesitancy in accepting the call. I prayed earnestly about the matter and felt definitely the leading of the Holy Spirit in the acceptance of the call. Even then, deep down in my heart, was the hidden yearning to see the little group reunited with the mother church one day.

Somehow I could not bear to think of the division continuing forever. It haunted me, at the close of the day, to think back on the morning when I had seen two brothers pass each other, going in opposite directions to church—one of them to direct the Bible school in the Grace Church and the other to direct the Bible school in the Covenant Church. Although the brothers worked side by side on their farms during the day, without mentioning the affair, somehow I felt that there had to be a lesion there, a suppurating wound in the heart of each that somehow must be healed. Having had no previous experience in such a situation, I tried to live one day at a time, leaning heavily upon the Lord.

Frankly, I do not think that I ever preached to a more appreciative audience than I found among the members of the Grace Church. Nor was I ever surrounded, up to that time, with more love and understanding. It was a type of friendship and love that made each gathering a happy experience to remember.

It was evident that God's hand was upon the church as we gathered for worship from week to week. God was moving among the people as if preparing them for greater joys in his service than they had ever known before.

On one Sunday in particular, it seemed that we were all gathered with Jesus on a spiritual mountaintop. One of the brilliant young girls in the church, Pearl Lee, the daughter of the local physician, Dr. Richard Lee, and his beloved wife Ruby, stood before the congregation at the time of the hymn of invitation to give a testimony.

The week before, she had written the pastor a long letter telling of her experience at Ridgecrest and of her feeling that God was calling her into a special work among the mountain people. Pearl was a recent graduate of Blue Grass College and had made an outstanding record there as a student, though she was one of the youngest to graduate from the college up to that time.

It is easy to see her now, in the mind's eye, as she stood before the congregation that morning recounting, slowly, and with queenly poise, the call of God that had come to her to do mountain mission work. Some of the words of her testimony I recall, vividly, to this day. She said in substance, "All of you here have known me since the day of my birth. Many of you cradled me in your loving arms when I was an infant. You were here at the time of my conversion, and you were present when I was led down into the baptismal waters. All of you know, I believe, that since the day I yielded my life to Christ I have tried to live faithfully as his child; I have tried to follow his leading in every area of my life.

"But last week at Ridgecrest," she said, "something wonderful happened. A great change came over my life. God seemed to speak to me in a way that I could not fail to understand, saying, 'You are to go on a mission for me . . . you are to serve me as a chosen vessel!' "

This is what happened in the life of Pearl Lee. That fall she enrolled in the WMU Training School of Southern Baptists at Louisville, Kentucky, where she began to prepare herself for her life mission.

Not long thereafter, Pearl asked me for an appointment there at the Louisville seminary, where I was fellow in New Testament Greek, saying that she had something very special that she wanted to talk over with me. I was there in Room 4, Norton Hall, waiting for her at the appointed time. She came right on the hour, but not alone. By her side, and walking hand in hand with her, was a brilliant young ministerial student, Ronald Sims. This was the first inkling I had had of the romance, but I sensed it immediately as I looked on their faces as they sat side by side there in my small office. Laughingly, Ronald said to me, "I am in love with this girl, and I want to marry her, but she tells me that she wants a career!"

My reply was, "Why, man, her career is already cut out for her: It's to be your wife, and work side by side with you as together you serve the Lord."

Following their marriage, they went out together to a Tennessee church to serve until God called them to Green Hills, Kentucky, to pastor the First Baptist Church and lead that church in one of the greatest home mission programs that the mountains of Kentucky or any other part of our land will ever know. At one time the church was sponsoring eight or more preaching stations, all of which later developed into thriving churches.

And so the work went on in the little Grace Church with joys without measure. But underneath the waves of joy that touched our hearts were the dark waters of an undertow that seemed to jerk me away from the shore into a depression that was almost overwhelming as I fought to surface again. In truth, I knew something had to be done. I knew that this terrible lesion that had come into the spiritual life of the community had to find a healing. It simply could not go on forever!

As the time came to leave for the summer vacation, there was a burden on my heart that was indescribable. By reading medical literature, I know something of the symptoms of angina pectoris and of coronary thrombosis. I think I could almost describe, in medical terms, the pain syndrome that marks such illness.

Something akin to this, by analogy, affected my spiritual heart and, it seemed, my whole body. I knew that on this vacation I would have to gain both physical and spiritual strength and the assurance of spiritual guidance, or else I could not go on with the burden.

One day after reaching the mountains, I went apart to pray as Jesus taught us. There upon my knees I cried out to God in the agony of spirit, pleading with him to show the way, to make it clear so that my young and inexperienced mind could follow it without error. I told the Lord that I did not think that physically I could go on without his presence and his guiding hand. "Please show me the way, dear Lord," I said. "Please show the people the way, and prepare them, and prepare me to lead them so that this awful illness may be conquered."

When the season of prayer was over, the burden was not gone. But for the first time I felt his living presence in such measure that I knew I would be able to go on, and that one day his holy purpose would be worked out in all our lives. In a word, I had "the blessed assurance." I knew that God was going to fulfill his holy promise to work with us in all things unto good—with those of us who love him and are called according to his purpose (Rom. 8:28).

Leaving what to me was little less than my "burning bush" on the mountainside that August morning, my wife and I returned to resume our studies at the seminary and to take up the work again at the Grace Church.

Somehow the days had already become brighter for me as I thought about the future of the Grace Church and of the Covenant Church. It is difficult to explain the feeling that seemed to come over me. At the moment, I could not see the way. I did not know how the transformation would take place. There was no blueprint for the human eye to see, but inwardly I was aware that the finger of God was tracing out on his drawing board the course of the future for the two churches. I knew something was going to take place. God had assured me there was a better way!

Day by day, guidance seemed to come from God. First I began to talk to the people about having a daily Vacation Bible School the following summer when all of the children of the Redbud Community and the Brunswick Community (about four miles away) might join together in the effort. Although I proposed that the Bible School be held on neutral ground at the Brunswick Church, there was instant dissent. I felt the flak of unknown voices. The word would come to me of how this one had said so-and-so in dissent, and another one had said thus-and-so! But the congregations involved finally gave assent for all the young people to work together in a Vacation Bible School. Somehow I felt that if we could accomplish this objective, it would be a starting point toward something greater and better along the road to unity and understanding.

When the Bible School was over, I proposed to the people of Grace Church that we undertake to have a joint revival meeting, having the day and night services alternately at the two churches.

It was a long, painful road to achievement. First, I merely introduced the matter and asked the people to think about it— the people of both churches. I did not want them to act upon it on the spur of the moment. I wanted them to consider the matter until they felt they could give such a joint revival effort their hearty assent and cooperation; otherwise, a real spirit of revival would be lacking.

Finally both of the churches agreed that they would undertake such a revival, although the pastor of the mother church had already resigned his work there, and the church was without a pastor.

After much prayer, the Lord led me to approach Dr. J. McKee Adams—professor of Biblical Introduction at Southern Seminary, a very godly man and deeply spiritual, about coming to preach for us during the revival. I laid the whole matter out before him, as best I could, and asked him to pray about it. After he had given me his answer as to his willingness to come, I proposed to the two congregations that they extend him an invitation to lead both of the churches in revival along the lines suggested.

When Dr. Adams came to lead in the revival, the people, somewhat reluctant at first in their support, began to manifest a growing interest in his messages, and it was obvious that the spirit of revival was descending upon the people. Dr. Adams was particularly well-prepared as the preacher for that particular revival. As all who knew him would say, he was an extremely warmhearted man with an outgoing personality. He was also deeply spiritual and had that rare capacity to live the message he preached. Doubtless many of his students will recall now that in some of his class lectures at the seminary, when he was dealing with subjects of archaeology, the scenes were literally made to live, and the characters of those faraway days and faraway places seemed actually to walk before us. We could almost hear them breathe, and see their footprints! The congregations were captivated by his messages. He preached Christ with power, and his reliance upon the Holy Spirit was evident from the beginning.

On Thursday evening before the last night of the revival, I left home, following the evening service, and told my beloved wife, Fern, not to look for me before morning: I was going out to join two deacons in a night of prayer.

Going to the home of deacon David Johnson, we were joined by his cousin John Johnson, and together there in the living room of the Johnson home, we began to read and to pray together. I had felt led to call upon these two men to join me in the night of prayer because both of them were godly men and upright in all their ways. Both of them were veterans of World War I, and both of them knew how to stand up in a crisis without flinching. In their company I had spent many an hour, but not once had I heard either of them speak of anyone in the community in an unkind way. I knew they were true believers in the Lord Christ. I knew they believed in prayer and the power of prayer. I knew that they would spend the night gladly in supplication to God for the healing of the hurt of the churches and the community.

For the reading we turned to the Book of Acts and began to read and to pray. One would read a chapter, and then there would follow a season of quiet meditation, and sometimes sharing in spiritual conversation. Then we would pray. Each one would take his turn in reading. Each one would take his turn in prayer. Each one would take his turn in spiritual conversation relating to the passages of hope which we had just read.

At the first appearance of light in the morning, I walked toward the window that lay toward the east, looked out upon the faint tinge of rose in the eastern sky, and stood watching until the first rays of the morning sun began to be perceptible. Then I turned and walked back to the center of the room where, by then, my two brothers in Christ were standing, and said to David, "David, how do you feel after our night of prayer?"

He replied, "I feel like God has heard our prayers and that all will go well." Then I said to John, "John, how do you feel?" He answered, "I feel the same!"

Then I spoke, saying "God has heard our prayers. His miracle will take place."

That evening at the worship service, the proposal was made and voted upon by the church that the Grace Church be disbanded and that each member of the church be granted a letter to unite with the church of his choice, but with the earnest and prayerful plea that all members of the church return as one to the mother church.

Already the proposed action had been discussed with the representatives of the mother church. And the congregation there had voted to accept any and all who would return, with a pledge never to reopen the wounds of the past, never to discuss again the things that had led to the division, to strike from the minutes all references to the lesion, and to bury all references to the matter forever in an unmarked grave.

Following the vote of the Grace Church where there was no

opposition, but merely a few abstentions from voting, we had the benediction. Then the people began to come up, one by one, to ask that their names be placed on a roll of those who would go back to the mother church. But all of this took place only after much prayer had been made to God in humble petition for him to give all the right spirit so that healing would come to all the body of Christ.

There was much weeping and crying that night. Men embraced men, and women embraced women, amidst tears of joy.

But there were three strong families that did not come forward to signify their willingness and desire to return to the mother church with the group as a body. One by one, the following day, I visited these friends.

The first one was the family of an elderly man who lay abed with a grave illness that was soon to take him from our midst. After recounting the amazing work of the Holy Spirit in bringing us to a near unity, and after a long season of prayer, as I knelt by his bedside, he raised his hand and said, "We will go back, too!"

To the second home I then went, where I sat down in the living room with the father and mother and their children. We talked at length concerning the course that the church had decided to embark upon in the effort to effect a true reunion of all the believers. Misgivings were voiced freely. And some doubts were raised as to the possibilities of a fruitful, effective reunion of the bodies.

After much conversation, and reasonings, I asked the father and the mother and the sons to join us in prayer on our knees. Then I called upon one of the sons to pray first, for somehow I felt the unspoken longings of the heart of the lad for all of the church families to be back together as one. His prayer of petition to God literally melted all of our hearts. There was no ground left to stand upon in dissent, or to kneel upon, when his prayer was over. Then I called upon the father to pray, and then the mother, following which I brought the prayer to a close.

As we arose from our knees, the head of the household, a

giant of a man in stature, and one of the noblest and most upright souls I have ever known, took my right hand and buried it in his big hands, rough from the labor of the field, and said to me, with his eyes in tears, "We will go, too!"

Then I made my way to one of the oldest farmhouses in the community, the home of Joe Bright, a former sheriff of Lake County. A beautiful home it was, of brick that had been painted red, with all of the wood exterior of the building neatly trimmed in pure white—a spacious home in which I had broken bread again and again, and where I had experienced some of the most gracious hospitality that a pastor could know.

As I drove up into the yard of the home, I saw "Brother Joe" carrying two buckets and headed toward the hog pen which lay between the house and the barn.

Upon seeing me, he set down the buckets, grasped my hand, and waited for my first words. As I spoke to him of the decision of the other members of the church to return to the mother church in reunion, he said to me, "No, I have been in this enough, I believe; I do not want to get back into such a situation again!"

I began to entreat him to go with us so that we might make the effort unanimous in our hope of letting God use us, lead us, and guide us all as one group again, through the coming years.

Still, he was adamant in his position.

Then I said, "Brother Joe, you will not mind if I pray, will you? And you will join me in prayer, will you not, that God's will may be done?"

Quietly he bowed his head as I prayed.

When the prayer was ended, he said to me, "I will go for your sake."

To which I answered, "No, Brother Joe, not for my sake. If you cannot go for Christ's sake, the going will have no meaning!"

"Uncle Joe" (as many called him) was a man who did not shed tears easily. He had served Lake County as a high sheriff and was known for his strength of character and rugged determination. He was a man whose mind, once set in a given direction, was not easily changed. He was an individualist in the strongest sense of the word.

After pondering my last words to him for moments, he turned and said to me, "Then I will go on the terms you suggest. Pray for my boys!" With these words, his voice choked and his eyes filled with tears. Another prayer followed then, and we shook hands and parted.

This meant that all seventy-three members of the Grace Church would go back together as a body, and this they did.

In the meantime, the mother church, which was then without a pastor, hurriedly called a meeting of that body where it was proposed that the young pastor of the Grace Church be called as pastor of the Covenant Church and consequently as the pastor of the reunited church. A unanimous call was extended and was accepted by the Grace pastor, who was also invited to move into the parsonage which stood on the opposite side of the road and just to the east of the church.

From the moment my wife Fern and I entered the parsonage, we felt surrounded by arms of love. The people filled our pantry with canned goods from their cellars and from the fruits of their toil.

Early in the first week of our stay in the parsonage, a large Kentucky-cured, country ham was delivered at our door. Two or three days later another ham came. And so it was over a period of many days—there would be a gift, and another almost identical would follow, each group seeking not to be outdone by the other in expressions of love for their pastor who had led them in coming together. That was the only sign of the fragmenting of the congregation that was left. The issue was buried completely in an unmarked grave!

There are some scenes on earth that cannot be described. One could never describe, adequately, the feelings of the mind and heart of a young lover who looks for the first time into the captivating eyes and face of the girl that one day, he is resolved, will be his wife. One can no more describe such a moment than the artist could portray with black oils, on a canvas, the soft radiant colors of a sunset. It is something that the lover is aware of, but that he could never describe. So it was with the reunion of these two churches.

Late one afternoon soon after the two congregations had been reunited under the compulsive persuasion of the Holy Spirit, I looked upon a scene that I cannot forget while there is memory.

Just beyond the church, to the right, and looking toward the west, lived one of the central figures in the controversy, Bill Flint. Although advanced in years, he was still active as a farmer, and virile and buoyant in physical strength. His spirit was clothed in a rugged body of almost giant stature. His shoulders stooped slightly from years of honest toil. He emerged from the front door of his home, walked down the steps and out onto the roadway that led to the post office.

As he entered the roadway, his eyes turned to the left where another man, likewise a central figure in the controversy, was walking in the same direction. They had been on opposite sides in the matter—completely opposite.

Flint paused and waited for his neighbor. I do not know what words passed between them as they joined each other in the roadway, but I saw them as they started off together, walking almost in military fashion—in perfect cadence.

In a moment, I saw them move closer together. The left arm of Bill Flint moved gently until it circled the waist of Jim Dougan, and then the right arm of Jim Dougan moved until it circled the waist of Bill Flint.

They walked toward the west, bathed in the soft rays of a sunset such as I had rarely looked upon before. I knew then that the vessel "made of clay" that had been marred in the hands of the potter had been made over again as it seemed good to the potter to make it (see Jer. 18:1-6)!

8

The Joe Brown Story

The most amazing instance of answered prayer that I have experienced, I share with you in the Joe Brown story that I now relate.

On a typical weekday afternoon my telephone rang, and the voice on the other end of the line said, "Can you come to the hospital quickly? Joe Brown is dying, and the family needs you!"

Instantly, I hastened to the hospital. Rather than wait for the elevator, I climbed the steps to the second floor and went directly to Brown's room.

It was an unforgettable scene. The nurse in the room was merely keeping watch while the patient lay on the bed with the sheet drawn neatly to the chin, with the face exposed, and his eyes open as if staring at the ceiling.

As I entered the room, the nurse arose and, glancing toward Joe, shook her head and raised her hands with that gesture of total abandonment that is so common to a scene like that when all efforts to save a life have failed.

"The doctor has just left," she said, "for there is nothing more that can be done. He's gone!"

Why I would have questioned those fatal words, I do not know, but somehow I wanted to look and see for myself before going to console the mother, who was waiting in a nearby room.

Now I know about death—the death symptoms. A doctor friend gave me a lesson on the signs of death one night as we stood by and watched one of his patients go. He showed me how there is a total absence of reflexes. He spoke of the ghastly pallor that spreads over the face and the entire body. He carefully pointed out how the pupils of the eyes begin to dilate until they achieve the fixed position. He called attention to the icy, glassy, meaningless stare that marks the eye as death comes on.

First I noted the fixed eye, and saw the dilated pupils and the icy stare. I saw the pallor that had already enveloped the face. Still, I placed my warm cheek just over the nostrils and mouth of the body so as to see if I could feel any sign of breath. There was none.

When I pulled the sheet down, exposing the upper part of Joe's body, I saw the left arm, with multiple breaks, lying there almost in the form of a swastika. Joe was riding a motorcycle at the time of his accident, I was told, and somehow lost control and crashed into the supporting structure of a power line. The result of the impact had been terrible!

Placing my right ear close to the chest over his heart, I listened intently to see if I could sense any evidence of a heartbeat, or a tremor—and there was absolutely none. Then I felt for a pulse, but found none.

Turning the sheet back up as it was, I said to the nurse, "Where is the mother?"

She replied, "She is just across the hall in the room that is next to the one facing this one."

Sadly I left the room, searching as I walked for words that would be appropriate in my effort to console the grief-stricken mother.

As I entered the room where the mother was waiting, I found her standing in the center of the room with her head down and wringing her hands in silence.

What word I spoke first to her, I do not recall; I only know I was astounded at her response, and totally unprepared for the words she spoke to me. I only know that she looked at me with staggering amazement, and with a face that was lined with such concern as I had never beheld on a woman's face.

Instantly she interrupted me, saying, "What are you trying to tell me? You are not saying to me that Joe is dying—that he is dead! He cannot be dying—he cannot be dead!

"From the day Joe was born, I have prayed, asking God to let him live, and to let me live, until he comes to know Jesus. Joe doesn't know Jesus. He can't die now! God has to answer my prayers. He has to keep his promise. He can't let Joe die now."

Upon hearing the words of the mother, I offered no more words of consolation. (I had spoken only a few words, for the moment the mother sensed the motive of my mission, she interrupted me with her inflexible affirmation of faith in the ability of Jesus to keep her son from dying.) Rather I knelt at the mother's feet and began to pray. How long I remained in prayer I do not know. I only know that as I prayed, I was caught up in the Spirit, and I wept profusely, beseeching the Heavenly Father to turn back the cold tide of death which, according to the words of the nurse and my own observation, had already swept over Joe.

It was an agonizing experience. Being familiar with the words of Jesus, and the basis of answered and unanswered prayer, I was in no position to question as to whether the mother had fulfilled those conditions. I could only think of the words Jesus spoke in response to the entreaty of the centurion of Capernaum who came beseeching him to heal his servant who lay at home sick of the palsy, grievously tormented, and how he said, when he heard of the centurion's faith, "Verily I say unto you, I have not found so great faith, no, not in Israel" (Matt. 8:10, ASV).

The story of the days that followed is too long to relate here. It is enough to say that Joe Brown did not die! He lived! What was thought to be the end was only an interval of silence, for the signs of life, so strangely absent a short time before, returned to the body that had felt the chill of the wintry blasts of death. Joe Brown lived and got up from what was thought to be the bed of death to walk again, yea, to walk down into the baptismal waters of testimony to a growing faith—a faith such as he had first beheld in the life of his beloved mother.

And the Claxton Funeral Home did not come for Joe Brown's body, as planned. Rather, Joe Brown later became an ambulance driver for the Claxton Funeral Home.

There are many other instances of answered prayer that I might relate, for all through my ministering years as a servant of God, I have believed in answered prayer and have practiced, assiduously, a day-by-day life of prayer.

And long ago I learned the secret of answered and unanswered prayer as I pondered some of the great texts of the Bible on prayer, and more especially the words of Jesus, such as those in John 15:7. Indeed every major decision in my life has been made only after hours of intercessory prayer.

Still, it is not the long hours of praying that determine the basis of answered prayer—not that! But there are times in our lives, as children of God, when it is necessary for us to tarry long in prayer so that our minds and hearts may become perfectly attuned to him whose word of instruction we await. When Jesus said, "If ye abide in me, and my words abide in you, ask whatsoever ye will, and it shall be done unto you" (John 15:7, ASV), I think he meant just that. If Christ is to give us guidance in hours of need, then we must become a suitable dwelling place for his words; and he must become, in spirit and in truth, our dwelling place.

It is interesting to note that Charles B. Williams translates the passage, "If you remain in union with me and my words remain in you, you may ask whatever you please and you shall have it." The ancient Greek word which Jesus used, and which the King James Version translates "abide" and Williams translates "remain in union with," means literally to sojourn, tarry, remain, abide. The idea is that of remaining in a place without departure, for the verb has the sense of continuing to be present. Where the time element is emphasized, it means to continue to be, not to perish, to last, to endure. When used of persons, it may convey the meaning to survive, or live.

In a word, once a person comes to be "in Christ," he remains in that estate (abides in it) and Christ's words likewise abide in him.

This, to me, is the foundational basis, the primal requisite, for answered prayer.

9

One Man Finds His Lord

A friend from seminary days was pastor of the Green Ridge Church and invited me to assist him in a revival. He endeavored to acquaint me with the type of opportunity that I would have during the revival. The church was made of faithful, churchgoing people whose lives, for the most part, were morally upright. But there were individuals in the community that the church had never been able to reach. One of these persons was a young man of great ability whose life had been lived wholly apart from the church. One of the church members, in speaking of him, said to me, "If you can win Jim Smothers to an acceptance of Jesus as Savior and Lord, Mr. Caudill, all of the effort put forth in the revival will have been justified!" Jim was a man, they said, who had absolutely no use for preachers, and wanted nothing to do with them nor with the church!

Jim Smothers began to burden my heart. He was on my mind day and night during the first two days of revival. All the time I was trying to figure out a way to meet Jim and to know him personally.

One of the neighbors said Jim was a great squirrel hunter. Although the forests round about were full of squirrels, he was a man who would hunt for hours to get a single one. He was a good marksman and loved to hunt, just as many men love to play golf or ply the quiet waters of the sea offshore with a sailboat. Consequently, I asked a neighbor if he would contact Jim and tell him that the preacher was a man who loved to hunt and see if Jim would be interested in taking him squirrel hunting.

As a boy in the Blue Ridge Mountains, I learned to hunt quite early and enjoyed hunting as perhaps no other sport at the time. I became a fair marksman—and still am, as those who have hunted with me in later years will testify. Only recently at a turkey shoot in the mountains I chose target No. 13 (which no one else seemed to want) and had the good fortune to make the best shot (though I had not fired my shotgun for a long time) in a field of twenty-five who were competing for the turkey! But I was not at all interested in squirrel hunting, as such, during the revival. I merely wanted to use the hunt as a means of getting to meet Jim Smothers on common ground.

The neighbor contacted Jim, and he said quite readily, "Sure, I'll be happy to take him squirrel hunting!" I suppose he thought it was unusual to find a preacher who could shoot and who was interested in hunting squirrel. The whole thing struck a very responsive note with him and he was ready and happy, it seemed, for the experience.

He was as cordial as anyone I had ever met, and we started out at once, without dialogue, on the quest for a squirrel. I watched him closely as we walked through the woods, and I saw at once that he knew his way around in searching for a squirrel.

He had the footfall of an Indian. I watched him as he lifted his feet and put them down softly—especially if he detected a sound that he thought might have been the barking of a squirrel. I could see, also, that he was slow on talk as we moved along. A good squirrel hunter would never, on the hunt, engage in much conversation. He knows that it is necessary to walk stealthily and to be as silent as possible, if he is to approach a squirrel that is feeding or lying in the sun on a limb.

Here and there in open places, as we walked, we would talk. Little by little I began to "inch around him," as we used to say in the mountains, in conversation that slanted toward Jesus and the church. Almost invariably, he would endeavor to deflect me from the course of my conversation, and at times he would change the subject abruptly. I was unable to get him even to pause for a moment and think on my words about Jesus. He seemed determined to stay away from all thoughts that had to do with Christ or the church.

So it was, for hour after hour, as we tramped through the woods.

Late in the afternoon, the dog treed a squirrel. Hurriedly we made our way to where the dog was barking, and found that the squirrel had entered a hole in the decayed portion of the trunk of a large oak tree some ten feet from the ground. Jim knew his dog well enough to know that he had located the squirrel and that it was in the tree.

As we stood there gazing up the tree, the Lord prompted me to make a direct thrust at the mind and heart of Jim concerning Jesus and our need of him and his life-style in our day.

Strangely enough, Jim turned and looked straight at me as he placed the butt of his gun stock on the ground and held it by the barrel, as if to say, "Well, go ahead; I'm listening now. If you have anything to say, say it!"

Never have I been more conscious of the Holy Spirit's presence and of his promise to "convict the world in respect of sin, and of righteousness, and of judgment" (John 16:8) than I was there as I talked face-to-face with Jim Smothers.

At first, as I spoke, his eyes were squinted as he looked at me with a sort of stony glare—as if he were thinking, "Well, you think you have me cornered, don't you—something that no one else has ever done! But I'm going to let you go ahead, just to hear what you have to say."

If my life depended on it, I do not think I could recall many of my words to Jim, but this I know: I was led in the words I spoke by the directing power of the Holy Spirit. God put in my mouth, on that eventful afternoon, the words I should speak to Jim.

Of course I began by telling Jim what Jesus had meant to me. That is the place for every person to begin in his effort to win a follower to Jesus. I talked about Jesus both as a man and God— and how he lived on earth. I almost delivered a lecture in Christian apologetics, always coming back to our personal need for Jesus as Savior and Lord of our lives.

Little by little, I could detect the barriers going down in the mind of Jim. His eyes lost the critical, querulous squint, and he opened them up as if to say, "Go ahead—I'm listening to every word you say; just keep talking!"

How interesting it was to look into his eyes as he opened them up full and wide. They were beautiful and seemed to have a depth of understanding that was far beyond the ordinary.

One can tell so much by the eyes of a person. One can tell if the person is alert, or sluggish and lethargic. One can tell if the mind is bright, or if it is dull and stupid, just by the glint of the eye. One can tell if the person is warmhearted, or cold and stonyhearted by the stare of the eye!

But Jim Smothers' eyes had, by now, become warm and beautiful to look upon, and I realized that the Holy Spirit had, at long last, given me full rapport with him.

As we stood on the southeast side of the old oak tree, a terrible rainstorm came up. Before I realized it, we were both drenched to the skin. Honestly, I was not even aware of an approaching storm, and I do not think Jim was. But there we stood, motionless as milestones, and literally drenched with a hard-falling rain, and there the dog was, with his floppy ears, still sitting on the ground with his nose pointed up the tree, uttering never a sound. We all must have looked as though we had been sculptured of stone and placed there as a monument.

Finally the moment of decision came, and I said to Jim, "Jim, it's a yes-or-no matter; I have to speak like that to you. You have always been a man of decision. You have been that way about the church, about Jesus, about your work. You have been that way about preachers!

"You think, I know, Jim, that I have trapped you into this position, and maybe I have!

"After all, it really wasn't a squirrel hunt that I wanted; I wanted to get to know you. And I wanted to come to know you for one reason, Jim, and no other: I wanted to be able to talk to you about Jesus and ask you if you would open the door of your heart and let him come in so that you could become his follower, his disciple—henceforth.

"Will you do this?" I asked. "Will you open the door of your heart and let him come in? Have you the courage to say to the Lord, 'Lord, I know I am a sinner, but I also know that Jesus came into the world to save sinners, and I want you to save me. And if you will save me, Lord, I pledge to you that I will follow you and try to live according to your commands as long as I live'?"

By now, Jim's eyes had left my eyes, and his face was turned toward the ground. But I am convinced he was not looking at the ground. He was looking into eternity and wondering what it would be like to die without a Savior.

Realizing that this man could not be pressured too much, I said to him, "Jim, you do not have to give me the answer now. After all, the answer you give to my question is an answer that you must give to God, for I am only an instrument of the message.

"And, Jim," I said, "may I urge you to think over all that has taken place this afternoon—my words to you, your thoughts in response to my words—and then see if you can work through this maze of indifference, and indecision, and receive Jesus as your Savior and Lord!

"May I entreat you to come to the service tonight and listen to these words once again as I preach and endeavor to point the way more clearly to those of you who do not know Jesus."

By this time it was well past five in the afternoon, and it would soon be time for the evening service.

Without any firm assurance one way or the other, we parted. I will never forget the handclasp he gave me and the look from his eyes. I knew then that I would see him at the evening service.

As I rose to preach that night, I located Jim on a pew near the rear of the church and just to the right of the center aisle.

As I preached, I was strangely aware of the Spirit's presence. It seemed again that I was being led in every word of the message—led by the Holy Spirit—and I could see that Jim was listening intently as I dealt with sin and held up Jesus as the Lamb of God that takes away the sins of the world. My words seemed literally to cascade as a stream of water dashes over the rough rocks of the waterfall in its quest for the sea.

When the invitation was given, the first person to step out and come forward was Jim Smothers. I remember how he walked. There was no hesitation in his steps. He was all bent forward, as a runner would bend, face downward, till he reached where I stood. Then his big hand went out, and his face turned up toward mine as he said, "Tonight I become a follower of Jesus. From this day on, my life is in his hands!" The whole congregation was visibly shaken as the people witnessed what was taking place.

The whole service was a Holy Ghost experience, but no part of the service surpassed, in the Spirit, what took place at the close of the service. Here is the story.

The pastor and I tarried in front of the pulpit, after we had greeted the people and bade them good night—those who came up to talk about the service and to ask us about our plans for the following day. Presently Jim Smothers, who had been standing all the while near the front door, came bounding up the center aisle, his eyes streaming with tears. He grasped me by one arm, and the pastor by another, and said to us, "Come and pray with me. I've got friends who are just like I was, and I want you to pray for them that they too may be saved."

Instantly we all knelt together as the words of our prayers, both uttered and unuttered, went up to God in the midst of a torrential downpour of the Holy Spirit.

Now the pastor knew, and I knew—and all who were present

at the service that evening knew—that Jim Smothers was a saved man, no longer to be numbered among the lost of the Green Ridge community; and the saving was the result of the work of the Holy Spirit. The guest evangelist was only an instrument in the great transformation that took place in the life of Jim Smothers.

10

The Holy Spirit and Church Renewal

When I concluded my ministry of thirty-one years at First Baptist, Memphis, and took leave of my dear people there, an interim pastorate was the farthest thing from my thoughts. I did not dream that I would ever serve anywhere as an interim. My plans were to return to the mountains of western North Carolina, where I grew up, and to write and engage in preaching opportunities on Sundays, and mission work in general among the mountain churches, as God might open the door. I promised him that I would enter such doors as opened and serve without reference to what the given situation might be able to do for me personally. I also promised the Lord that I would enter the doors in the order in which he opened them for me and in such places as he led me to see the greatest need.

Almost instantly upon arrival at our mountain home, which is located some fifteen miles west and slightly to the north of Boone, doors began to open on every side, and choices had to be made. In each choice I endeavored to keep faith with the promise I made to the Lord as I left the Memphis pastorate.

Early in December of 1976, a long-distance call came from a pulpit supply committee in another state, asking if I would consider coming and serving as the interim supply for the church during their quest for a new pastor.

The pastor of the church had given up his work some sixty days before, and the church, according to the committee, desperately needed an undershepherd who could be on the field during the period of search for the new minister.

At the moment I had no desire to go. I had never thought of doing interim work anywhere. But after talking with the committee at length, I agreed to pray over the matter and to consider earnestly the invitation.

In the meantime, another call came from the committee saying that the church had voted unanimously to invite me to come to them as interim pastor. With this call, I knew that I should go to the work there, for in "putting my fleece out," one of the stipulations was that the church call me without a single dissenting vote. For that matter, that has been a part of my "fleece" in every call I have had. The first question I would invariably ask, "Was the call unanimous? Was there a single dissenting vote?"

On January 14, Mrs. Caudill and I arrived at the church to take up our work. Immediately we were confronted with the fact that there were serious divisions within the church membership. Although a large congregation was present at the first worship service, I was aware of the tension that prevailed. It came to me from many sides. At points there was bitterness and ill feeling between members of the congregation. Word of the division within the membership had reached me in North Carolina before accepting the call, and this is one of the things that made it very difficult for me to give an affirmative answer. Never had I been associated with a pastorate anywhere that was marked by division, and the long years in the pastoral calling were not enough to deliver me completely from an apprehensive mood as I considered the work there. The experience I had had at Redbud, Kentucky, in pastoring a splinter group that had moved away from the mother church was with a completely united group. Within that little body there was a sweet fellowship and a close spirit of unity.

But here was something different—a church that was not actually "split" in the sense that a group moved away to form a new church, but a church in which a great number of members were so fragmented in their relationships with each other that some had actually left the church, while others remained in the church but without reconciliation.

The key to the mood of reconciliation, I believe, was found on the night (past the midnight hour) when I met with the pulpit committee to consider the work as interim pastor. It was around ten o'clock when I reached the airport, and my host brought me immediately to the church where the entire pulpit committee was in an upper room waiting for my arrival. For almost two hours, I counseled with the committee on procedures in the call of a new minister, for this was the primary reason for the meeting of the larger group. Without formal preparation for such an hour, I spoke with complete liberty, summarizing, point by point, some of the chief facets of consideration for the pulpit committee in their quest for a minister. There was a time of give and take as questions were freely asked, and the interrogators turned to me for answers. Well past the midnight hour, something wonderful took place—something that set the mood for all of the work of the committee henceforth.

In speaking frankly with the committee, I said to them, "You would indeed perceive me to be a naive person in the assumption that I am unaware of some of the tensions that exist among you incident to past events. Let us not attempt to recount them or the basis for them, for my word to you tonight concerns reconciliation. You will not be able to make yourselves available for the Spirit's leadership unless each of you is first reconciled with God and then with one another.

"If there are differences among you (and I must say frankly that I assume there are differences), are you willing to put those differences aside for the sake of the great cause that brings you together?

"Where such differences tend to exist among those who profess to be followers of Christ, I know of no way to resolve them except upon the knees of prayerful petition to God and with a forgiving spirit."

Then I said to the group, "Is each one of you willing here

tonight 'to forgive and to forget' past differences and to turn to one another and say, 'I ask you to forgive me for any word that I have spoken that has brought hurt to you, for I forgive you of any word that you have spoken that has been hurtful to me'?"

I went on to say that when such forgiveness comes, the basis of the misunderstanding and the hurt should be buried in an unmarked grave and never discussed again. Then I said to them, "Those of you who are ready and willing and desire to forgive and to forget all past differences from this day on, and who will endeavor to be motivated by the love of Christ in every interpersonal relationship, will you join hands with the ones on each side of you and kneel as I kneel now for a season of prayer to our Heavenly Father?"

For a long time we were on our knees as one after another prayed in a great outpouring of the heart to the Heavenly Father.

When the prayer was ended, and we arose from our knees, all standing in a circle, I was conscious of the overwhelming presence of the Holy Spirit. I knew from the prayers, and from the tears that fell, that all had experienced a glorious sense of reconciliation.

Upon my return to North Carolina, and a few days later, I received a call from the chairman of the pulpit committee, saying, "Dr. Caudill, something wonderful took place the other night when we were on our knees with you at the committee meeting. Up until that time, as chairman of the committee, I was only able to moderate." (And at that point he spoke of the crosscurrents he had had to deal with in every committee meeting, and of the impossible mood of things.) "But after the night we went down on our knees together, everything was different! From that moment on, every meeting has been conducted with a sweet spirit of unity, peace, and understanding. Surely God has taken over in all of our lives!"

In the first meeting with the deacons of the church, the chairman, a distinguished educator of years, and a very perceptive man, said to me, "Pastor, we are here to do God's will under your leadership. You tell us what to do and give us guidance. We are ready to follow."

And that was the mood of the deacons during all my days in their midst. And that was the rule of the finance committee as they met together, from time to time, under the duress of a budget where the income of the church was not adequate for the stated needs.

Some of the members of the church indicated to me, privately, their apprehensiveness at the first business meeting of the church. I can recall so vividly the feeling that I had as I stood before a group that had been marked by great dissidence at earlier meetings and literally prayed throughout the conference for the Spirit of God to lead and to guide. Little by little, the mood of disagreement began to disintegrate and vanish. Clouds of uncertainty were gradually dispelled. Words of apprehensiveness became more and more infrequent in the day-by-day endeavor of the church. A mood of optimism began to prevail among the members of the pulpit search committee and spread throughout the membership, it seemed.

Then, on a memorable weekend, the chairman of the pulpit committee informed me that the committee would like for a church conference to be called so that they might make a report to the entire congregation. The chairman informed me that the committee was united, completely, in their desire to bring before the church their recommendation.

Prior to the church conference, the committee chairman indicated his desire, and the desire of his fellow committee members, to renew their vows to God and to pledge to the church their love for the Lord and for one another, and their desire, henceforth, to be reconciled with him and with one another for all the days to come.

On the following Lord's Day, and at the close of the morning service, the chairman of the committee came forward and handed me a statement neatly typed out in which he declared, as an individual and as a member of the pulpit committee, his desire and the desires of the committee members to renew their vows to God and their love for one another in the name of Christ. Then one by one the members of the committee came forward, took my hand, and paused by my side as we looked out on the immense congregation that was gathered.

Very quickly I moved back to the platform. Looking out upon the people, I asked them if there were those of the congregation who were members of the church and who would like to join in this affirmation of reconciliation in which we had been led by the committee, saying, "Those of you who would like to make this same affirmation of reconciliation and love for God and for one another, in the renewal of your own vows to God, please join hands with one another and move in a series of concentric circles around the walls of the sanctuary."

Quickly the members began to move out and join hands until circle after circle stood around the walls until there was room for no more. Then I noticed the people in the pews begin to join hands with one another until, it seemed, almost the entire vast assembly stood clasping one another's hands in a covenant of love and reconciliation such as I had never witnessed before.

It was a soul-shaking experience and one that I shall remember, vividly, forever. In all of my experience as a pastor, I had never seen anything like it. It was a real-life drama in which the Holy Spirit came down and baptized, it seemed, the whole body of believers with the Presence.

When the service was concluded and there was time for reflection upon it, I thought, "Surely I have witnessed today a scene such as was common to the New Testament Christians in the long ago. Surely this, in a sense, was Pentecostal!"

On the appointed Sunday, and following the hour of worship, the pulpit committee came forward to make the report in which each member of the committee shared. One by one, following the report of the chairman, the members gave their reasons for presenting to the church their recommendation.

After the Committee had made the report, the moderator gave

the congregation an opportunity to act upon the report. Instantly there was a move that the recommendation be accepted, approved, and that the prospective pastor be called.

As moderator, I remember how thoughts raced through my mind concerning the manner in which the vote should be taken. The suggestion had been made that the vote be taken by secret ballot, but somehow I felt that unless there was a move to that effect, we would take the vote otherwise. My decision was that the vote be taken by voice, with the people seated, for this would give any voice of dissent an opportunity to express disapproval without embarrassment. The voice vote was a resounding "yea." At the invitation for a negative vote, one or two very faint voices spoke in dissent.

Then I called for a standing vote on the part of those who would call the prospective pastor, and it seemed to me that the whole membership stood. Naturally, there were a number of visitors present who could not participate in the vote.

When those in opposition were called upon to stand, there was not a dissenting vote!

For some three weeks following the call, I remained on the field, endeavoring to help prepare the church, in a further way, for their years together with a new undershepherd.

As Fern and I journeyed homeward, less than a week before the date for the arrival of the new minister, I began to look back over the three months' experience. There was only one conclusion as I thought, and prayed, and rejoiced: I had witnessed the powerful presence of the Holy Spirit who had heeded, once again, the call of God's people in a great hour of need, and had come with his overwhelming presence to heal, to bless, and to restore. I knew I had experienced reconciliation in its most glorious expression!

11

Mending a Broken Home

Every time I think of what took place in the life of Joe Downy and his wife Sue, fresh hope comes into my heart—hope for the unnumbered thousands of homes throughout America that are broken or disintegrating under the pressures of contemporary society. These homes could be healed and restored to marital health and spiritual beauty, if both of the participants could find the courage to face honestly the issues that led to the crisis.

I was a complete stranger to Joe and Sue Downy until the Monday afternoon when they came to me for help. The couple lived in our city and had been outstanding citizens, but now their dreams were shattered, their hopes in despair, and their relationship split completely asunder.

Joe Downy came to my office alone, by appointment. Right on the minute, he walked through the door facing where I sat at my desk and made no attempt to conceal the deep surge of emotions that had brought him to my office.

No sooner had he sat down than he burst into tears and began to sob audibly. Many a man had sat in the chair where he sat, discussing domestic problems, but I had never heard a man cry as Joe cried. It was the cry of a broken heart.

For a few moments I waited, without a word, until Downy regained his composure. Eventually he looked up and said to me, "I need God!"

His words really shattered the silence, and I knew immediately that I was faced with a distraught soul that was in dead earnest.

As Joe sat before me, trembling with emotion, I waited for him to speak again. Frankly, at his first word I was not sure about the motivation of his sense of need. I did not know whether he wanted the presence of God merely to help him through some present difficulty, some material impasse, or whether he wanted God in his life for another reason.

My doubts were soon dispelled, for Joe Downy began to talk about his life—that he was a sinner and that he had failed God. After some time, almost incidentally it seemed, he brought in the matter of his broken home.

Joe's home was broken all right, but that was not the thing that seemed to be uppermost in his mind. His great concern seemed to be his spiritual condition.

Frequently in my years of ministry, I have seen both men and women under conviction for sin, but I think no one among them showed the painful remorse of past living more vividly than did Joe Downy. His soul was literally full of lament. "I have failed so miserably," he said. "I have failed God; I have failed my wife; I have failed my family; I have failed everybody!"

And then he went on to say, "What I need is God! I want you to tell me how to get God into my life. I want to make a fresh start, and I can't do it without help. Understand?"

Often I had thought of the words of Jesus in John 16:8 when he told his disciples that he was going to leave them. Actually his leaving would be to their advantage, for, said he, "If I go not away, the Comforter will not come unto you; but if I go, I will send him unto you. And he, when he is come, will convict the world in respect of sin, and of righteousness, and of judgment" (John 16:7-8, ASV). Goodspeed in translating the passage put it this way, "he will bring conviction to the world."

Here I saw this conviction taking place before my eyes. Here was a man gripped by the conviction of his sins and his lost estate. He was lost and he knew it! What is more, he was begging for help.

Times without number I have been on the begging end—

beseeching persons to consider Jesus as a means of changing their life-styles and coming into a better way of living. But here, I was on the receiving end; God allowed me to be almost as a bystander and witness the miraculous working power of his Spirit in the life of a sinner seeking forgiveness and grace to begin life anew.

Step by step, I endeavored to acquaint Joe with God's plan of salvation as the Scriptures set it forth. I explained the character of repentance and the new birth. We stayed for a long time on the words of Jesus to Nicodemus where he informed that brilliant inquirer that he could not even see the kingdom of God or enter it unless he were born from above, born of the Spirit.

Joe seemed to have a very keen mind, and it was easy for me to move from stage to stage in the presentation of the gospel. I knew from the way he gave assent to my words of instruction that he had evidently had some background of religious knowledge. He had at least been exposed to the gospel, and many of the things he had heard had evidently "sunk in."

It was not like plowing in a new ground. In cultivating a parcel of ground that has been recently cleared of trees, there are roots everywhere in the subsoil—roots to catch the blade of the plow, causing it to bounce back and fling the handle of the plow into the ribs of the man who is holding the handle. Often, in plowing through such soil, one has to "back up" and make the second go!

This was not necessary with Joe. I was able to plow a straight furrow right through the roots of his difficulty.

The real problem with Joe Downy was not to convince him that he was a sinner and needed a new life-style—that was not the problem. He had already come to that point before he entered my office. My problem was to help him lay hold of faith. He wanted to have faith, but somehow he did not seem to know how to do so.

All of which reminds me of an incident in the oral examination which I was required to take in partial fulfillment for the degree of Doctor of Philosophy in the field of Greek New Testament. Dr.

W. H. Davis, the chairman of the Examining Board, said to me, "Paul, turn to Romans 1:17, read the passage, and tell us what you think it means."

On the examination, all I had to read from was a copy of the Greek New Testament. I was told to bring to the examination a new copy that contained no marks of any sort—no notes!

Slowly I translated the passage, "For the righteousness of God is revealed from faith unto faith in it [that is, in the gospel, for the word "gospel" is the antecedent]." Then I went on to explain how, as Williams made it so clear in his translation, it is "the Way of faith that leads to greater faith."

Ronald Knox translates the passage "faith first and last"; whereas *The New English Bible* puts it this way, "a way that starts from faith and ends in faith." J. B. Phillips translates it "a process begun and continued by their faith"; the *Twentieth Century New Testament* reads "resulting from faith and leading on to faith."

At any rate, I was witnessing a vivid reenactment of the fulfillment of that premise. Joe had a measure of faith, or else he would never have come to the office of a stranger for counsel about his problem. But now his faith was growing, and I could almost see it grow as he sat open-eyed (and now clear-eyed), before me. Why, I could almost see the bud of faith opening up visually. It was like a photographic study of the growth of a flower that unfolds before the camera's eye.

Finally, I asked Joe if he would like to pray, and have me pray, for God to take away his sins. I read to him the words of the psalmist saying,

> Jehovah is merciful and gracious,
> Slow to anger, and abundant in lovingkindness
> He hath not dealt with us after our sins,
> Nor rewarded us after our iniquities.
> For as the heavens are high above the earth,
> So great is his lovingkindness toward them that fear him.
> As far as the east is from the west,
> So far hath he removed our transgressions from us.

Like as a father pitieth his children,
So Jehovah pitieth them that fear him.
For he knoweth our frame;
He remembereth that we are dust (Psalm 103:8, 10-14, ASV).

When Joe prayed, his words went out in earnest petition to God for forgiveness—for the privilege of starting a new life as a disciple of Jesus. He asked for mercy, and with a repentant heart he acknowledged his transgressions. He professed faith in Jesus and in his power to save him.

When the prayers were over, I arose first, and then Joe arose. Together we stood, face-to-face, for an instant, in complete silence.

"Are you ready to receive him?" I said. "Is it in your heart to become a disciple of Jesus for the rest of your days on earth?" (He was a mature man forty years of age, I suppose.)

No words of assurance were needed on Joe's part to convince me that here was a man who had passed from death unto life! The evidence was on every side. I could see it in his eyes, in his face, in his words.

Now he was relaxed. Now there was a glow in his eyes which were no longer racked with the pain of conviction for past sins. Now the assurance of forgiveness radiated from his face and through every word he spoke.

At this point we sat down again, and I asked Joe if there were any other personal problems in his life that I might help him with.

Immediately he replied, "Yes, I have an awful problem. My home is broken, and my wife and child are gone from me.

"But that's not the worst of it," he said. "My wife has obtained a peace warrant that forbids me from even approaching her, or going about the house where she lives, and where I lived until the crash came."

"Do you really love your wife?" I said to him. "Do you really want your home to be reunited? Do you love her enough to pay the price of making things right in every way? Do you think you are capable now, even with the help of God, of changing your life-style so that your home can become a viable place for your wife and daughter, as well as for yourself?

"Would you like for the three of us to sit down together and talk about the matter, and explore ways and means of a reconciliation, under God?"

With those words, his face lit up like a glowworm in the dark, saying, "Oh, if you could only do that. Do you think you can? Do you think it's possible?"

Picking up the telephone, I dialed the office of the local sheriff and related to him what had just taken place. Briefly I said to him, "Will it be all right with you if I call Joe Downy's wife and ask her if she would like to come to my office and talk about the problem between her and her husband with a view to reconciliation? Are you willing to trust the two in my hands in this way?"

The sheriff was instant in his response, saying, "Sure, go ahead. That will be fine!"

Fortunately, when I dialed the Downy home, Sue answered the phone. When I acquainted her with my reason for calling, her voice broke, but she quickly replied, "Yes, I will be happy to come. I'll come right now. I'll be there in minutes."

As Sue walked into my office, I invited her to be seated to the left of Joe in a chair which I had placed close to his chair.

The very minute Sue sat down, and before a single word had been spoken between us, she broke into tears, saying, "It's all my fault! It's all mine, I tell you!"

Joe offered rebuttal to her words, but Sue was adamant in her position, saying again, "I say it's all my fault!"

In a quiet, calm manner, I related to Sue what had taken place. I told her how Joe had come in and cried out for God's help, and I was glad to be able to tell her that Joe had not spoken a single unkind word about her. He had laid no blame at her door for what had taken place in their lives.

Attentively, Sue sat and listened. After a while she added, pensively, "We haven't had God in our lives. We've lived our lives alone. We have gone our own ways!"

There, in the holy quiet of that mountaintop experience, I saw another soul pass from darkness unto light—from death unto life! I saw Sue Downy converted just as her husband had been a little while before.

When we arose from our knees again (for I had prayed earnestly for God to make clear to Sue the way of salvation which I had so earnestly tried to relate to her, just as I had to her husband, and to give her the courage to do what Jim had just done), I was convinced that her conversion, too, was genuine. All sham, all hypocrisy, all deceit had been laid aside as filthy garments, and both of them stood there before me locked in the embrace of forgiveness and redemptive love.

Silently, I looked away as they caressed each other with sweet, forgiving words of love, for it was a scene too tender, too beautiful, and far too sacred to be shared.

For a long time I stood gazing out of the west window and thinking how wonderful it would be if both the husband and wife of every broken home in the nation could lay hold of the secret that had brought healing to the home of Joe and Sue Downy. What a change could be wrought, overnight, in the home life of our land.

Later Joe and Sue went down into the baptismal waters together, and together they began their new life in Christ Jesus.

One day, not too long afterward, Joe called me saying, "I have the day off, and I would like to come and chauffeur for you today, if it will be helpful to you."

Joe was in government service, and highly respected. He had learned that from time to time members of my congregation would come and chauffeur for me, especially in downtown calls. They would take me to an office building and then park the car and come for me when I was ready to go on my next call.

As we were driving down Airways Boulevard on a mission that day, Joe said to me, "Isn't it wonderful, Dr. Caudill, what God can do! God did it, didn't he?"

"Yes," I replied, "God did it through the convicting and healing power of the Holy Spirit."

12

The End of a Feud

This story has to do with a feud. The two families involved lived almost within a stone's throw of each other—certainly less than a half mile. One party ran a filling station, and the other party farmed and worked at various other trades. Both of the men were of strong build. One of them was Bill Cobb, of Irish stock, I believe; the other was Jim Bullis, of Dutch stock. No one ever told me how the feud originated. They only told me that it was in progress, for I was their pastor.

Previously, I thought the only place a feud took place was in the mountains, and I still recall some of the lurid stories I heard about feuds in the mountains of western North Carolina and eastern Kentucky.

Now a feud, as we knew it, was a bitter, growing hostility between two families or two clans. The point at issue might have occurred decades ago, but the hostility over the injury continued.

There were times when the feud resulted in deaths—sometimes multiple deaths. But bitter hostility was always present, smoldering, sharp, and unending. I remember hearing it said of one man, "That fellow would kill you if you made him mad enough, but he would never rob you. He might shoot you and leave you lying in the road, but he would never touch your pocketbook!"

As a college student and young pastor, however, I came to learn that not all of the feuds take place in the mountains.

Sometimes they are found in the Piedmont and the lowlands that follow in the slant to the sea.

One day the Cobb and Bullis feud came to a head: Jim Bullis pulled up to the filling station of Bill Cobb, turned off the ignition switch of his engine, and placed his hand on the door as if to get out.

Bill Cobb, who was standing inside his station watching Bullis, took a step forward, slapped his hand on his gun which was in a rear pocket, and said to Bullis, "You get out of that car and put your foot on this ground, and you will die!" Cobb gave no explanation beyond that, for he was a man of few words. As he stood there waiting, his face grew redder and redder.

Bullis, being a man with utterly no sense of fear, unlatched the door of the car, and was on the point of stepping out on the ground, but changed his mind and did not do so. Instead, he gave Cobb a long, icy stare, as if to say, "You think you've got me, don't you? You merely caught me off guard—that's all!"

Bullis started his motor and then sped away.

The incident was the talk of the town. The person who told me about it simply said, "We barely missed a killing this morning!"

"A killing?" I said. "What do you mean?"

"Well, you may not know, for you have not been here long, but there's been a feud going on between Jim Bullis and Bill Cobb for years. They literally hate each other—each hates the ground on which the other walks!"

When my neighbor had finished his story of the incident, I replied, "We've got to do something about this! We simply can't let this go on. They are both members of our church, and I am their pastor!"

My neighbor shook his head as if to say, "Well, I am sorry to tell you, Pastor, but things like this don't mend. They just go on till something happens."

The story cast a spell of gloom over me. I suppose I came as near being plunged into despair as I have ever been as a pastor.

Already I had come to love both of the men, and to think that
they were at odds with each other and giving way to hatred was
almost more than I could take.

After thinking over the matter for days, I had a conference with
the chairman of the deacons and insisted that we call together the
deacons of the church and ask these two men to appear with us
in the hope of effecting reconciliation.

Nothing like this had ever taken place in the little church
before, and I must confess there was a fainthearted response on
the part of the deacons as we came together on that weekday
evening.

At the hour set for the conference, one by one each deacon
filed into the sanctuary and took his seat and, at my suggestion,
near the front. Finally Cobb came in and took his seat there near
the front where most of the deacons were sitting. Bullis came in
last and took his seat on the opposite side of the aisle.

It was a meeting such as I had never attempted to preside over.
I knew nothing about procedures at such a time, except to rely
upon the Holy Spirit. I had read in God's word that in difficult
moments, if you rely upon the Lord completely, he will give you
guidance. That is the assurance Jesus gave his disciples, saying,
"And when they bring you before the synagogues, and the
rulers, and the authorities, be not anxious how or what ye shall
answer, or what ye shall say: for the Holy Spirit shall teach you in
that very hour what ye ought to say" (Luke 12:11-12, ASV).

I can hardly remember a word that was spoken that evening as
we began our conference. I only knew that it was a deeply
emotional experience and that I was caught up in the Spirit's
presence. I also know that the Presence gave me utterance so that
I could speak with freedom and confidence.

My heart was deeply burdened, at the time, with the feeling of
necessity for brotherhood among believers. I thought of the
words of John, "Beloved, let us love one another: for love is of
God; and every one that loveth is begotten of God, and knoweth
God" (1 John 4:7, ASV), and of the words of Jesus who said unto

his disciples, "A new commandment I give unto you, that ye love one another; even as I have loved you, that ye also love one another. By this shall all men know that ye are my disciples, if ye have love one to another" (John 13:34-35, ASV). With these two passages of Scripture as a basis, it was not difficult for me, in the space of a few brief moments, to lay on the hearts of the deacons and the offenders the absolute necessity for us to love one another.

Moreover, I recalled and shared with the group the words of Jesus who said in the model prayer, "And forgive us our debts, as we also have forgiven our debtors" (Matt. 6:12, ASV).

After a long season of persuasion in which the chairman of the deacons spoke and others expressed their warmhearted spirits of reconciliation, I turned to Bill Cobb and said, "Brother Cobb, will you forgive Jim?" To my question there was, at the moment, utterly no response. Bill Cobb merely stared out into space with icy eyes. He seemed rather to be lost only in the contemplation of what he was not going to do, for as I stood there in front of him, and very near, I could see determined opposition. His face was almost "as red as a beet," I thought.

Cobb was short in stature but very rugged in build. He had a frame that suggested the strength of an ox. As he sat before me, I could see the muscles in his neck literally bulge with anger and hidden resolve, and I heard him say half under his breath, "I'll never budge . . . I'll never budge an inch!"

Lost in my thoughts at the mental attitude that Cobb was reflecting, I had all but lost sight of Jim Bullis, who sat before me and to my left. I had already come to see, however, that he was a man who, in spite of the feud, might be a bit easier to reason with, and less fixed in his thoughts than Cobb. Though he was fiery and impulsive as a spirited racehorse, I had seen something in Jim Bullis that made me believe that he would be open to reason in our effort to effect a settlement.

Of course, we had prayed long that evening when we first gathered. We opened our meeting with prayer after I had commented briefly on the nature of the meeting, but now we were on our knees in prayer again.

How long did we pray? I do not know. No one bothered with looking at a watch that night. All of us had one burden—a common burden; all of us wanted reconciliation between two of our dear neighbors.

One after another the deacons prayed. One after another's tears fell on the floor like summer rain.

Finally, it came my time again to pray. As I knelt to pray, somehow I felt that my whole body, mind, and soul were at the point of being crushed in the vise of hatred and bitter contention that was going on between the two strong-willed men. I felt that I was directly in the line of fire, and I could all but feel the bullets of hatred whistle by me like shrill winds flying through the treetops on a cold winter night.

When the second series of prayer was ended, God gave me a flash of guidance—a moment of inspiration that I could never forget. His Spirit put in my mouth words that I had never before spoken in dealing with human problems, but which I have spoken countless times in the intervening years in efforts to heal the minds and hearts of those who have been bruised and separated by needless confrontation.

This is what I said to them: "God can and will heal your awful hurts if you will only allow him to do so. I come therefore to plead with you to forgive and to forget, and to bury your hatred for each other, and the objects of your confrontation, and your wounds, in an unmarked grave. Let us gather them all up here tonight and with our own hands dump them all into a grave in some obscure place where grasses grow, and let us neatly fill the grave with the fresh dirt and leave it there for the grass to cover—completely, without a marker, and never to be seen again!"

Then I called the people to prayer again, agonizing in a petition to God for complete reconciliation, for total forgiveness, for completely restored fellowship.

When the prayer was over, I extended my right hand toward

Bill Cobb and said to him, "Brother Bill, will you take the step first tonight in effecting reconciliation between you and your brother? Are you willing, on your part, to forgive, to bury your differences in an unmarked grave, and there to let it lie forever—even until Jesus comes?" Not spontaneously, but slowly, as if his whole frame were seized with painful agony, Cobb lifted his eyes toward me and, as a mist gathered in them, lifted his right hand, and finally extended it toward my outstretched right hand until our hands clasped.

Never will I forget that handclasp, for he was a strong man and had a grip like that of an iron vise. Overwhelmed with emotion, he gripped my right hand until he almost crushed the bones in it.

For some time Cobb stood there, looking straight into my eyes with his piercing dark brown eyes. Then suddenly, and with great feeling, he said, "I will!"

At Cobb's words, I burst into a prayer of thanksgiving to God that he had put it into his heart to forgive and to forget and to start a new life with his neighbor.

Turning to Jim Bullis who, quite obviously, was deeply moved by his erstwhile enemy's bold confession, I asked him pointedly the same question: "Will you, Brother Jim, forgive your brother here tonight, and on your part are you willing to take all of the injury and the wounds of the past, and the differences of the past, and bury them in an unmarked grave and there let them lie forever until Jesus comes?"

Almost instantly, the fiery, tempestuous Jim Bullis, whose mood reminded me so much of that of Simon Peter, sprang to his feet and offered me his hand, saying, "Yes, I will; I will forgive Bill, and I am ready now to start out new!" With his word, and still grasping his right hand, I reached for the right hand of Bill Cobb and drew it toward the hand of Bullis. All the deacons were standing by now, and the scene that followed was filled with heavenly glory.

As the two men stood face-to-face, clasping right hands in an unmistakable covenant of friendship and holy resolve to start life all over again as neighbors and friends, I broke out into song in which all joined, singing, "Praise God, from whom all blessings flow;/Praise him, all creatures here below;/Praise him above, ye heavenly host;/Praise Father, Son, and Holy Ghost."

As the little group filed out of the white clapboard church on the hill, we all knew that we had witnessed a miracle of God's grace. We knew that what had taken place was not the work of any human being, but of God . . . that the reconciliation was the work of the Holy Spirit who had visited us in almost undreamed of power in one of life's most crucial moments.

So far as I was able to discern, the feud between Bullis and Cobb was at an end, for their lives had been made over again by the convicting power of the Holy Spirit.

13

Witnessing in a Beauty Parlor

Chinatown, Los Angeles, was the setting for a glorious, memorable experience on a May morning in 1975. It all took place in a beauty parlor—and I had never been in a beauty parlor before for more than a moment.

Fern and I had left Memphis on Monday morning after my last Sunday as pastor of the First Baptist Church there. We went directly to Marco Island, Florida, where we were to spend a month at Sunset House North. There we enjoyed days of pure delight and experienced intellectual and spiritual growth as we read together, prayed together, gathered shells on the nearby beach from day to day, and completed the manuscript of my new book, *Changing Life's Style.*

Early in April we headed westward, visiting many places of interest which we had never visited before, among them the Painted Desert and the Yellowstone National Park. Upon our arrival in Los Angeles, we visited with Chinese friends briefly before departing by plane for Honolulu.

The morning before our departure, Fern decided to go to the beauty shop operated by Mrs. Shu Quan Wong, a Chinese lady whom we had previously known for years in Memphis and who was the wife of a US Air Force pilot who participated as a Flying Tiger in World War II under the command of General Chennault.

Since I was wholly unacquainted with Chinatown, I decided to go to the beauty parlor too and spend my time there reading as I waited for my wife.

Soon after I sat down in the waiting room and began to read, a lovely Chinese lady in her early thirties entered with an elderly lady and sat down nearby.

Having ministered to Chinese in both the Augusta, Georgia, and the Memphis, Tennessee, pastorates, I introduced myself and began to engage the young woman in conversation. I explained to her that I had just recently come from Memphis where, in the First Baptist Church which I served, I had received into the membership over two hundred Chinese, most of them by baptism. The young lady seemed to be greatly impressed with my concern for the Chinese, and from there on I found myself on common ground with her.

After a while I said to her, "What is your work?"

"I am a teacher here at the nearby university," she replied.

"And what is your field of teaching?" I asked.

She replied, "Biochemistry—I am a biochemistry major."

This led me to ask: "Where did you take your work, and what is your degree?"

She explained that she took her training at the University of Southern California and that she had received a Ph.D. in biochemistry.

For some time we talked about the character of her field of study. I had made a lifelong study of words and am a student of both the Greek and the Latin languages as well as of some of the Romance languages. So we discussed the meanings of some of the words most commonly found in her work. She seemed greatly interested in word study, but admitted that she had not given much attention to it in the field of her endeavor.

The study of the classics—Greek and Latin—is invaluable to anyone who is interested in the original meanings of words. For instance, if one were to delete from Lincoln's Gettysburg Address all of the words that stem from Latin origins, he would have great difficulty in understanding its message.

After a while, I turned to the young lady, who seemed to have a brilliant mind and to be far above the average in refinement and social manners, and said to her, "Do you know Jesus?"

Cordially she replied, "I do know something about him, for I have read a part of the New Testament and know something of his ministry."

Then I asked her if I might share with her my own experience with Jesus and tell her how he had come into my life and brought to me the greatest blessings I had ever known.

From the moment that I mentioned the name Jesus, I detected a marked interest on her part. I thought I observed in her face something of a keen desire (if not an eagerness) for me to go on with my story.

Sensing her Buddhist background by her conversation, I began to speak in the manner of the Christian apologist, but very soon I spoke in a straightforward manner of my conversion and what it had meant to me to know Jesus as Savior and Lord.

Throughout the conversation, the young lady listened intently, hardly turning her eyes away. I noticed also that the lady by her side was listening intently too.

Verse by verse, according to the Scriptures, I related to her the plan of salvation—but not until I had first discussed with her, at some length, the basic premise of the New Testament concerning sin and the Savior. After all, how can one come to know the meaning of Jesus and to understand his mission on earth if he is not aware of the meaning of sin.

In detail I explained the meaning of conversion and discipleship. I read to her the words of Jesus as recorded by Mark who tells us that Jesus came into Galilee preaching the gospel of God, and saying, "The time is fulfilled, and the kingdom of God is at hand: repent ye, and believe in the gospel" (Mark 1:15, ASV).

Carefully I explained to her the meaning of repentance and how it calls for the alteration of the total life-style of a person—a radical reversal in the mood and manners of one's life. I explained to her that this change is a tripart change—a change of the mind, a change of the heart, and a change of one's conduct. I endeavored to make it clear to her that in receiving Jesus, one actually has to come to think differently about sin and about right and wrong in the light of the Scriptures, and that one must not only think differently but also feel different about sin and about righteousness. Then I explained to her that the whole course of one's life henceforth is to incline to the way of Jesus, for the Jesus way involves a completely new way of living—a new way of thinking, a new way of feeling, a new way of acting.

By this time, close to an hour had elapsed since we first began to talk. Realizing that my opportunity for pressing the question of commitment to Christ might soon be lost, I looked directly at her and said without apology, "Would you like to receive Jesus as your personal Savior? Would you like to become a follower of his—a disciple—and endeavor to achieve the new life-style which he declared is to mark the lives of all his followers?"

To my joyful surprise, she readily indicated that she would love to do so.

Step by step I endeavored to acquaint her with the meaning of such a commitment, explaining that it is a lifelong matter and should embrace every facet of one's life. I explained to her, in the words of James, how the Bible teaches that the followers of Christ are to be not only persons of inner peace but also people of outer service. The Christian, I told her, is first and foremost a person of faith, but there is more to one's relationship to Christ than mere faith; a Christian must also be a person of works, even as James said, "Wilt thou know, O vain man, that faith without works is vain" (Jas. 2:20).

As we talked together, I thought how stimulating it was to be able to talk to a person so completely literate (and with such unusual refinement) on such a theme; for she seemed to grasp with understanding every word I spoke and to perceive every nuance of thought which I directed toward her. I could tell that she was drinking in, and that with understanding, every phrase and every clause I uttered.

At length I turned and said to her, "Would you allow me to pray, right now, and will you join me in prayer, for God to help you begin your discipleship here and now?" Modestly, she gave her assent to my question, and I arose to pray, oblivious to those who came and went there in the waiting room of the beauty parlor. Standing with bowed head, I prayed earnestly for her conversion. As I concluded my prayer, I asked the Lord to give her not only the ability to perceive the plan of salvation which I had faithfully tried to outline to her but also to grant her the capacity and the determined will to make a decision to follow Christ then and there.

When the prayer was over, and while I was yet standing, I said, "Will you now confess your faith in Christ, and surrender your life to him from this moment on until the end of your days on earth? And in doing so, will you commit yourself to follow him in baptism and church membership at your earliest opportunity?"

Instantly she replied, "This I will do! I know of a Chinese Baptist church nearby, and I will go there and present myself to the church as one who desires to become a follower of Jesus."

As we both stood, with clasped hands, I prayed again for the Holy Spirit's seal of approval on the resolve she had made and for the Spirit's guidance during her period of adjustment as a new follower of Jesus.

After we had sat down again, I turned to the lady accompanying the younger woman and asked her if she had listened with understanding to the words that had passed between us. She indicated firmly that she had and added, "She is my daughter, and I would like to join her in the resolve that she has made today. I will accompany her to the church and will likewise present myself as one who desires to follow Jesus and be baptized into the membership of the church."

The joy I knew in the moments that followed cannot be described, for I had seen a beautiful young woman and her mother pass out of the darkness of unbelief into the gracious light of the Christian faith. And I knew also that I had seen two souls pass from death unto life!

As Fern and I left the beauty parlor, I related to her the joyful experience that I had just had, and we both marveled that the Holy Spirit could guide and bring about such a glorious conversion in the waiting room of a beauty parlor, as people came and went, and where, we surmised, up until that time, no prayer had ever been spoken!

14

Homesick and Homebound

On a hot summer evening in Augusta, Georgia, the rain had been coming down in torrents all evening. The humidity was high, and there was no air conditioning in the First Baptist Church where we had gathered for the worship service. We did have electric fans, however, that rested high on pedestals and were placed at convenient locations in the sanctuary to help make the intense heat of the summer evening more endurable. A few of the more affluent homeowners had installed air-conditioning units in their living rooms, but so far as I know, there were no central units yet installed in the homes, and none in the churches.

When God called me to the pastorate there, Fern and I spent our first night in the home of a neighbor who graciously cared for our every need. It was my first time to spend a night, however, in such a hot, sultry climate. Having been reared in the mountains of western North Carolina, and accustomed to cool nights, I pitched and tossed all night long because of the oppressive heat. I thought to myself, "I know God knew what he was doing when he called me here to serve as pastor, but really he's just about done me in, for I know it is going to take me a long time to get accustomed to this oppressive heat!"

One summer evening, for greater comfort, we had left the two main church doors open throughout the worship service—the doors of entrance from Greene Street which the church house faced.

The theme for the message that evening had to do with sin and

113

the Savior. All through the service I was deeply conscious of the Spirit's presence. I did not "want" for words, and it seemed that God was with me from the moment I began to preach until the last word of the sermon was spoken.

Every minister of the gospel knows that there are times, in proclamation, when one is especially conscious of the Spirit's presence and guidance in the words he speaks. At times, no matter how well the sermon has been prepared, fresh, new, gripping thoughts come to the preacher's mind, as he speaks— thoughts that may be extremely relevant to the message and to the occasion. It was such an evening of proclamation at First Baptist, Augusta, when, early in the service, a stranger walked quietly into the church and took his seat.

Throughout the service, however, I thought no more about the stranger. I just endeavored to preach as God gave me utterance.

After the hymn of invitation, and the benediction, I walked quickly to the center aisle entrance in the hope that I might greet, among others, the stranger who had come in. After all, I was attracted to his presence in an unusual way as he entered.

There was a large attendance that evening. As people came by to exchange greetings, I kept my eye on the visitor who was making his way toward the door. He seemed to be avoiding me, for I merely got to touch his hand as he hurried through the doorway and departed in the rain.

As the man went out, I got a clear view of his face, and I saw there a troubled brow.

Following the worship service, I went home, along with the family, and immediately went up to my study where I reviewed the evening service, and made out my schedule for the following day. A little later, I was interrupted by the voice of our young daughter who said, "Daddy, there's a man down here who says he wants to see you!"

"Show him up to my study," I replied, "for I will be happy to see him right now."

The man who entered was a tall man of large frame. His hair

was sandy in color, and he had a strong profile with features that bore a resemblance to the classic sculpture of the face of a Greek male.

At my invitation, he sat down on the couch in my study, and I went over and sat down by his side. (I thought it would make the conference a bit more informal if I sat on the couch beside him rather than in front of him—looking out over the desk.)

As soon as the man sat down, he said, "My name is Luke Edwards, and I want God!"

Edwards then dropped his head, buried his face in his hands, and began to cry.

I waited for him to speak, but there was no response. Then I said to him, "What is on your heart? Share with me your problem, for I assure you that you can talk with me in perfect confidence."

This is how Luke's story went:

"I am a married man, and have a lovely wife and a precious nine-year-old daughter. But I am separated from them and have been so for months."

Edwards spoke at some length of the separation and told how he had gone from bad to worse until it seemed to him that his life was beyond recall!

"Yesterday morning," he said, "I left my boarding house in Philadelphia, and started driving south. I had no place in particular to go. . . . I just wanted to get still farther away from things.

"Late this evening," he continued, "I drove into Augusta. As I passed the corner on which your church is located, I saw that the lights were on, the front doors open, and that a service was in progress.

"Why I went in," he said, "I do not know; but something seemed to draw me toward the church. Consequently, I parked my car and entered for the service."

Then he said, "What you said tonight in your sermon about sin and the Savior turned my life completely upside down. I am a lost man, and I need God! Can you help me find him?"

Feeling that it would be helpful to know more about Luke Edwards' life, and the circumstances that brought him to my house, I said to him, "Would you like to tell me more about yourself? Tell me about the things that led up to your separation from your family!"

The story that he related to me was a sordid one. It was another case of a man drifting in sin until he finds himself far out at sea in a self-made craft that is sinking!

At this point, Luke drew from his inside coat pocket a letter and said to me, "Here, read this!"

The letter was from his mother, and her words went something like this: "Dear Luke, I do not know where you will be when you receive this letter, but I want you to know that my love and my prayers are following you, and they will continue to do so."

As I read the letter (a very long one), I could see, here and there on the pages, splotches of teardrops. It was packed, from beginning to end, with the emotional pleadings of a mother's love.

"You will come back, one day," she said, "I know. God will bring you back. And I will be praying for you, son, day and night until you return."

When I had finished reading the letter, I returned it to Luke. As I did so, I thought of the words of Kipling in his poem, "Mother O' Mine."

> If I were damned of body and soul,
> I know whose prayers would make me whole,
> Mother o' mine, O mother o' mine!

Luke did not go into detail about his past life, for I did not encourage him to do so. I did not think it was necessary for him to do this, but he did tell me of certain events in his life. He had left his family in Connecticut and drifted southward where he found, for a season, short-term employment. But all the time, he explained, he was merely running away from the issue which, in his words, was "my own life of failure." He spoke of his wife only in the kindest of terms and seemed to want to lay no blame at her door.

As he spoke of his little daughter, I could tell that there was still in his heart a great affection for her. He spoke of her love for him, and of how he felt she must be missing him, even as he was missing her!

As I sat there looking at Luke, I tried to visualize his little daughter back home and to frame in my mind her thoughts as she longed to see her father and waited for him to return. I could imagine her saying, "Mama, where do you reckon Daddy is tonight? Do you think he will ever come back? Isn't there something we can do to find him and get him back? I love him so much that I don't know if I can stand it if he doesn't come home."

Then I could imagine the mother saying to her little girl, "Darling, whether your daddy will come back or not, I really don't know, but I believe he will. You know, dear, Daddy is a troubled man. He has some problems that he has not been able to conquer, and I really feel that he is not trying to run away from us, but to get away from his problems. This is why he has brought us so much sorrow. He still loves us, I know. No one could make me believe anything else. Some day, darling, I believe Daddy will be home again. We will all be together. It may be better with us than it has ever been before. Won't that be wonderful?"

Beginning with the verses that speak of sin—its character and its wages—I read God's Word to Luke, holding the Bible close to him so that he could follow my reading intently with his own eyes.

These are some of the passages I read: "For all have sinned, and fall short of the glory of God" (Rom. 3:23, ASV); "For the wages of sin is death; but the free gift of God is eternal life in Christ Jesus our Lord" (Rom. 6:23, ASV); "But what saith it? The word is nigh thee, in thy mouth, and in thy heart: that is, the word of faith, which we preach" (Rom. 10:8, ASV); "Behold, I stand at the door and knock: if any man hear my voice and open the door, I will come in to him, and will sup with him, and he with me" (Rev. 3:20, ASV); "For by grace have ye been saved through faith" (Eph. 2:8-10, ASV); "Jesus came into Galilee, preaching the gospel of God, and saying, . . . repent ye, and believe in the gospel" (Mark 1:14,15, ASV).

After the reading of the Scriptures, I asked Luke if he would like to kneel by my side and join me in prayer to God that he might experience forgiveness and the new birth of which Jesus spoke in his words of Nicodemus: "Verily, verily, I say unto thee, Except one be born anew, he cannot see the kingdom of God" (John 3:3, ASV).

Luke indicated his desire to repent and to believe and lost no time in getting down on his knees by my side.

I prayed first, as I usually do in such a situation, and then I called on Luke to pray. His prayer was a prayer of repentance and of faith from beginning to end. His words of confession fell from his lips, even as the raindrops of a storm fall upon the earth below. As I knelt by his side listening to his prayer of petition, I was convinced of his earnestness and of his sincere desire to be saved from his miserable past. I knew that here was a man who, with the deepest desire of his heart, was looking up to God for cleansing, for peace.

And peace came!

As we rose to our feet, he was rejoicing and saying, "Thank God, I've found him. I've found him! And I have peace!"

After a pause, we sat down again, and I said to him, "Luke, what do you want to do now?"

He quickly responded, "I want to go home. I want to see my wife, my daughter, and my mother! And I'm going. I am going to leave right away!"

Then I said to him, "Would you like to speak to your mother over the telephone before leaving?" He replied, "I would like very much to do so."

"Come, then," I said, "and we will go back to the church, to my study there. Then you can talk with your mother by telephone before you leave."

Actually, there was a double motive in going back to the church: I wanted to get a new copy of the Bible to give Luke—a Bible with some special passages marked for him to read along the way. I wanted also to arrange for him to have some money for the journey and to have the tank of his car filled with gasoline before leaving.

Upon reaching my office, I dialed the telephone number he gave me, and on the first ring, I heard a lovely, refined voice answer.

"Mrs. Edwards," I said, "this is Paul Caudill of Augusta, Georgia, the pastor of the First Baptist Church here. Your son was in the service this evening, and he has had a wonderful religious experience. He has found God, and he is coming home! He will be leaving here in a few moments. I wanted you to know, so that you might pray for him along the way."

Already the mother was sobbing (I could hear her clearly). So I said to her, "Yes, Mother, this is for real. It has all happened just like I told you!"

Then I turned and said, "Luke, would you like to speak to your mother?"

Luke took the telephone but was only able to speak one word, "Mother!" With that, he began to sob and handed the telephone back to me to complete the conversation.

First I placed in Luke's hands a copy of the Scriptures with markings on the fly leaf for him to read, and then I placed in his hands $25 (for he had told me that he was totally without funds). He tried, however, to impress upon me the fact that he had not come to me for that kind of help.

Then I called the Gulf service station on Broad Street where I usually bought my gas and asked the night operator if he would be kind enough to fill the tank of Luke's car with gas and give him a change of oil, and an extra can of oil for use on the journey, and charge it to my account.

After another season of prayer and words of friendly counsel, I told Luke Edwards good-bye and watched him depart in the rain which was still falling heavily—homesick and homebound, but no longer sinsick!

A few weeks passed and I heard no more of Luke Edwards, though he had been on my mind almost constantly. Then one morning a long letter came from Luke telling of his arrival home and of the joyful reunion that had followed.

In closing the letter, Luke expressed the hope that one day he might return to Augusta, the place of his conversion, and to the First Baptist Church and bring with him his beloved mother, his wife, and his daughter so that together they all might share with me their newfound joys!

As I laid the long-looked-for letter aside, I knew that Luke Edwards was a twice-born man. The Holy Spirit had once again fulfilled the promise of Jesus to convict the world "of sin, and of righteousness, and of judgment" (John 16:8)!

15

The Holy Spirit and Death

There is perhaps no experience known to human beings quite so enervating as watching another human being die. This is especially true when death comes to a friend, or even a distant relative, but when death comes to a family and takes away one for whom the love of the family knows no bounds, the whole physical body of the bereaved one may become so weakened by emotional trauma as to be all but overwhelmed by boundless sorrow.

But such need not be the case with believers—with those who have come to know the Lord in an intimate, personal way and have walked and talked with him during the debilitating interval that marks the decline of the loved one and the approach of death. The Holy Spirit has promised to be with those of us who know him in such times of sorrow and to give us the grace and strength we need, not only during the final crisis but also in the countless days of adjustment that follow.

The writer of the Book of Hebrews was aware of this Presence and had evidently experienced such in a marked degree. How else could he have said, "For we have not a high priest who is unable to sympathize. . . . Let us then with confidence draw near to the throne of grace, that we may receive mercy and find grace to help in time of need" (4:15,16, RSV)?

The story that I here relate is very personal, and intimate, and will never be told without its pathos. But it is a true story and one that I must share.

There was nothing unusual about the birth of Joseph Hardy Miller III. He was born as many other children, in answer to dreams and happy longings—as any child should be. The first word of his birth reached me by long-distance telephone. I was in New York City, having just arrived by a Pan American clipper from a flight across the sea. As soon as I boarded the DC-7 American Airlines flight for Memphis, I asked the stewardess for a postcard and addressed what I hoped might be Jody's first piece of mail. He was our first grandson.

While the birth of Jody was marked by no unusual experience, very soon in his life he became, in the eyes of the family, a very unusual child. There seemed to be an innate desire in his young mind and heart to do that which was right and proper. He was obedient to his parents, and although he was the second born (there were three girls and three boys in the family) he began, very early in life, to exercise a growing concern for his brothers and sisters. At times he was almost supervisory.

Jody became an idealist. He was a patriot at heart. He had no patience with the flag burners and with those who went AWOL. He felt that we are all to be involved in the support of our country, whether in war or in peace.

Jody wanted to prepare himself and go to Washington to serve his country. He was determined to be a lawyer, and he had decided that he was going to help right some of the wrongs that he felt so keenly exist in our land. He had read the inaugural addresses of all our presidents.

At school he took his studies seriously. He was an "A" student. He needed no one to prompt him to study, for he turned to his studies at night as normally as he walked to the table for food at the evening meal. Anything that fell to his hand, he tried to do it well!

Jody was an athlete. He had an exceptionally good stroke in golf and played with the best of his peers. He loved football and hoped that he might participate in that sport, come college days.

Jody was a leader at Central High School in Memphis. He ran

for the office of commissioner of student activities in his soph-
omore year, and lost. There was no bitterness in his loss; he took
it like a man, saying, "I will run again next year."

Jody did run again next year, but for the presidency of the
student body of Central High. During his campaign, I stopped by
his home one evening and found there a host of his supporters
from the school, both black and white. They were planning their
campaign and carefully staking out every procedure in their effort
to elect Jody. They followed those procedures and won with an
overwhelming majority.

But something dreadful began to take place in the physical
frame of Jody. Something was obviously wrong, but no one
could tell just what. He began to tire more easily. Then there was
pain. The pain first surfaced, acutely, on a golf trip on which he
was accompanied by some of his fellow golfers. He found it
difficult to compete in the game because of the pain. A lameness
began to develop in his right leg and hip.

Upon his return home, he was placed in the hospital for
extensive tests, and eventually there was a surgical procedure
which uncovered a condition in the pelvic area of the right hip
that raised suspicions. Still there was little to suggest what was
soon to follow. When his brothers came to the hospital, there was
a lot of joking about his stay there. No one took it seriously.
Everyone felt that things would soon be all right.

But things did not go well. The weakness, the pain, and the
soreness did not subside as was expected.

He was provided a used four-wheeled postal vehicle painted in
patriotic colors. His father thought that Jody might use it to drive
back and forth to school and to share rides with some of his
classmates. His father hoped Jody might find in it an avenue of
personal pleasure. The vehicle, with its fresh paint job, and the
new upholstery and repairs, was an impressive looking little
outfit. And Jody was as proud as pie of it, for it helped to mark his
sixteenth birthday.

But Jody got to drive the car only a few times. The necessary manipulation of his right foot and hip, in driving, brought him too much pain.

Very soon, Jody's father placed him in the Saint Jude's Hospital for further tests. After days of observation and study, they found the cause of the malady, and that was for the parents and family the shock of the years!

The news came to me early one morning when Joe, our son-in-law and father of Jody, called me from his office saying, "Papa, are you dressed?"

"No, not really," I replied. "I just have on my old jumpsuit."

"Just come right on to the office as you are, will you?" he responded.

Without the slightest idea of what was in store, I drove hurriedly to his office. As I entered the door, I saw our oldest daughter, Netta Sue, sitting with her face in her hands, and the father, sitting at his desk, in a dejected mood.

Joe's first word was, "We have just received the report on Jody, and it's bad."

At the moment, I knew nothing about Ewing's sarcoma. Although I had in my library Cecil's *Textbook on Medicine* and had read about many of the incurable diseases, I knew nothing about Jody's disease.

At Saint Jude's Hospital, they did all that mortal hands could do for Jody. Everything that the modern schools of medicine had to offer, and the latest in the medical arts dealing with Ewing's sarcoma, was used to help Jody, but to no avail. Each day Jody seemed to worsen. Little by little, his appetite failed, and he began to lose weight. One could clearly see that the pains of death were laying hold of him.

One evening I went in to see Jody alone in his room at the hospital. While there, I said, "Jody, there is a passage of Scripture that I would like to read to you, and I would like to tell you about my response to that passage, from time to time, as a minister."

I said to him, "Jody, you know I am here in a dual role tonight. I am your grandfather, but I am also your pastor and friend. I want to read this passage and then ask you what you want me to do about it."

This is what I read: "Is any among you suffering? Let him pray. Is any cheerful? Let him sing praise. Is any among you sick? Let him call for the elders of the church; and let them pray over him, anointing him with oil in the name of the Lord: and the prayer of faith shall save him that is sick, and the Lord shall raise him up; and if he have committed sins, it shall be forgiven him" (Jas. 5:13-15, ASV).

After reading the passage, I said, "Jody, there have been times when I have anointed the sick, and prayed, as the passage here suggests. I remember one case where healing came. I remember another instance where healing did not come. You know, Jody, you are a very sick boy, but you know also that our Heavenly Father is the Great Physician, and he has all authority and power. He can heal where medicine does not heal. He can lift up where all other help fails! Now if you would like, I would suggest that you share this passage with your father and mother. And if, after doing so, and after your own reading and prayerful meditation, you should want me to anoint you in this special way and to gather with others to pray for you, then you will tell me, and I will do so."

Like a flash, Jody said, "Papa, let me see that." I handed him the book which he took in his pale, frail hands, and for moments he was lost in reading the passage and in the pensive thoughts that followed.

Then he quietly turned to me and said, "Papa, I want that!"

The following evening, we gathered in his room—his father and mother, his other grandfather who was also a minister of the gospel, along with two of our beloved deacons of First Baptist (both of whom are medical doctors) who were in accord with James' words in the passage about prayer and healing.

Prior to the service I had gone to the drugstore and obtained a small bottle of olive oil. At the time of the ritual, I touched his brow, his chest, and his hip with a bit of the oil taken from the bottle and placed on the fingers of my right hand. A reverent hush fell over all of our hearts as we knelt to pray.

Joining hands in a circle around the bed, and with the parents holding the hands of Jody, one by one we prayed.

Just before the prayer, I read the words from John 15:7, saying, "If you abide in me, and my words abide in you, ask whatever you will, and it shall be done for you" (RSV). Then I added, "Here, as I see it, is the basis of all answered prayer. And may we all make the fulfillment of this premise our first resolve as we pray."

The burden of my prayer was this: "Lord, thou knowest how much we love Jody and how deeply we desire to see him raised up again in health, good and strong. We want him to be able to run, and jump, and play as he used to do on the fields of athletic contest. We know, dear Lord, that thou hast the power to raise him up. All authority is thine, both in heaven and in earth. Thou art able to raise the fallen when all other help has failed. We beseech thee, Lord, to give him back his health. But, dear Heavenly Father, should it not be in thy plan for his life, and for ours, to restore him to the fullness of health, we pray that thou will help us to love thee more and to serve thee better, for this is our resolve, and this is our prayer, in Jesus' name."

Day by day, we continued to pray, seeking to fulfill, in every possible measure, the words of Jesus in John 15:7.

Following his hospital experience at Saint Jude, Jody returned to his home and resumed his classes at Central. Eventually he could attend his classes no more, but his teachers allowed him to pursue his studies at home. He kept up his work and made excellent grades! From time to time his classmates would come by to see him, and one or two of them with whom he had special rapport would spend long seasons of fellowship with him in his room.

Finally the question was raised as to whether Jody should return to the hospital for some further treatment and care. He had already had the chemotherapy with all of its attendant discomforts. But Jody was adamant in his desire to remain at home.

As time dragged on, Jody grew perceptibly worse with each passing day.

A special reclining chair was acquired and placed by his bed so that he might be lifted into the chair for his periods of study and rest.

Each day he read his Bible, keeping it constantly by his side—that is until the last few days when his strength was at such a low ebb that he asked his mother to read to him the passage he would have read.

One morning when I was out making calls, a telephone call reached me, saying, "Papa, come quickly; something is happening to Jody. We need you!"

On entering the room, I saw there was a marked change for the worse.

Helplessly, we stood by the bed, waiting for the father, who was in surgery at that time, to come.

An effort was made to lift Jody up and place him in the chair, thinking it might afford him a little comfort, but the effort was an excruciating experience—for the pain was so great. Finally he was placed in the chair in the hope he would rest better.

Moments later, however, it became obvious that the end was near. That was around 1:30 PM. All afternoon, I stood by his side and hoped and prayed, praying silently much the same prayer we had prayed at the beginning.

Around 7:00 PM, Jody's mother said to me, "Papa, you have had no food since you came. There's food downstairs. Sandwiches have been prepared, and you must go down and eat a bite. You have been by Jody's bed practically all day!"

After further insistence, I went down for a sandwich.

What the family did not know was this: I had fasted all day long, praying earnestly for God to work a miracle and give us back, in some measure, the viable health of our grandson. Food was the least of my thoughts that day!

No sooner had I reached the dining room than one of Jody's sisters came rushing down the stairs and saying, "Papa, come, come. We think Jody is dying."

Sprinting up the long flight of steps to the upstairs room, I found the candle of life quietly going out for Jody. In seconds he drew his last breath and was gone!

Even with all of the advance warning, and an acute awareness of the impending crisis, we all stood about the bed stunned and speechless. Jody's brother, next to him in years, rushed out of the room, overcome with nausea. Now he realized that he would have his brother with him no more, for they were so close to each other—in all their thoughts and ways.

As soon as the brother regained his composure, he returned to the room where we all were still standing in silent sorrow around Jody's bed. It was then that I said, "Now let us read from God's Word and pray together for grace and help, even as God has promised, in this our hour of need."

Reaching for the Bible, Caudill, the brother who had been so sick a moment before, said to me, "Papa, I will read from Jody's Bible." This he did, taking the Bible and reading from it just as Jody had read so many times before.

After Caudill had finished the reading, I said, "Now let us all join hands and pray once again!"

In concluding my prayer, I said, "Dear Lord, now that thou hast not seen fit to answer our prayer, even as we know you were able to answer it, and now that we must part with Jody for the rest of our earthly days, we shall endeavor to live up to our covenant made with thee when we knelt about his bed there in Saint Jude's Hospital on that night of nights: we will try to love thee more and serve thee better!"

Then quietly, one by one, we began to leave the room as the ambulance came to bear Jody's frail remains to the nearby funeral home for the last earthly viewing. But as we tarried for a moment, following the prayer, I was aware of the presence of the

Holy Spirit in a measure such as I had seldom known in the hour of death.

Also, I was equally aware that in my own heart there was a deep resolve that would never leave me, namely, the resolve to love God more and to serve him better.

Jody's funeral was held in the afternoon so that any students who desired to attend the service might miss a minimum of their class assignments. Instead, the whole school was dismissed, and came in a body to Jody's funeral; for he was president of the student body, and this is what the students wanted to do.

At the graveside, besides the family and a host of friends from the church, there were Jody's friends from Central High. And in all of our hearts that day, as we left the tomb, there was a reverent hush and a deep silence such as only the conscious presence of the Holy Spirit can bring!

The next day, following the funeral service, one of Jody's teachers came to me and said, "Dr. Caudill, something wonderful happened today at school. One of Jody's young friends came to me in my office and said to me, 'From now on, my life is going to be different. It's got to be, for Jody's sake!'"

The Holy Spirit has been active in the lives of Jody's brothers and sisters. The witness of Jody's dedication to the highest and best impulses of life in Christ is reflected in their lives. The Holy Spirit that sustained him in courage, along with the tenderness of loving ministry by his three sisters and two brothers, has been a transforming work in each of them who shared the precious days with him.

PART II
Notes on the Holy Spirit

Notes on the Holy Spirit

Perhaps no phase of Christian doctrine has been so widely neglected by Christians in general as the doctrine of the Holy Spirit. At present, however, there is evidence of more than usual concern in the contemporary church for biblical doctrines as they relate to the Holy Spirit, and there is more than passing interest among the various religious approaches to the Christian faith in the charismatic gifts of the Spirit. But the majority of Christians, even today, give little evidence of a viable concern for the person, the presence, and the power of the Holy Spirit in our day.

Without any disposition to revert to the varied interpretations in relation to the doctrine of the Holy Spirit, let us briefly consider some of the more obvious biblical teachings concerning the person, the presence, and the power of the Holy Spirit, and how we as believers may come to know him and experience his presence in our own lives.

Any consideration of the Holy Spirit, of course, must begin with the premise that the world was created by God who, while dwelling apart from it as ruler and sustainer, yet dwells within it. Furthermore, "for a special purpose and in an appointed period of time he came into the life of the human race in the person of Jesus Christ, the eternal Son. That purpose being accomplished, God the Son withdrew to his heavenly throne to achieve the consummation of his work."[1] Then, so that God's presence might continue to be felt in the world and to guide and further the mission that his Son, Jesus, began during his earthly ministry, it

133

was necessary for the Holy Spirit to come as a person and abide among people.

Note

1. Harold W. Tribble, *Our Doctrine* (Nashville: The Sunday School Board of the Southern Baptist Convention, 1929), p. 58.

16

The Holy Spirit, a Person

The Bible consistently presents the characteristics of the Spirit as that of a personality. "The Spirit searcheth all things, yea, the deep things of God. For who among men knoweth the things of a man, save the spirit of the man, which is in him? even so the things of God none knoweth, save the Spirit of God" (1 Cor. 2:10-11, ASV). In Romans 8:26, Paul spoke of the Holy Spirit as one who makes intercessions for us "with groanings which cannot be uttered" (ASV). In Romans 8:27, he spoke of "the mind of the Spirit" (ASV). In Romans 15, Paul referred to "the love of the Spirit" (ASV) and entreated the Roman believers to join him in the fellowship of prayer. In Ephesians 4:30, Paul told of the response of the Spirit to human treatment, stating that the Spirit is grieved because of our unrighteous deeds. The offense of Ananias (Acts 5) was that of lying to the Holy Spirit.

Throughout the Bible the work of the Spirit is represented as that of a person and not of principle; as that of an individual rather than as a form of energy. He is held up as a person and "not merely a pervasive influence."[1]

Jesus invariably spoke of the coming of the Spirit in personal terms (see John 14:16-17,26; 15:26; 16:7-14). Paul spoke of the Holy Spirit as though he were a person (Rom. 8:26) and in Ephesians admonished his brethren not to grieve the Holy Spirit (4:30).

In Acts 8:29 it is the Holy Spirit that speaks to Philip concerning the Ethiopian eunuch and directs the evangelist on his mission. The Holy Spirit spoke directly to Peter (Acts 10:19), and to the church at Antioch saying, "Separate me Barnabas and Saul for the work whereunto I have called them" (Acts 13:2, ASV).

The Holy Spirit, therefore, should never be referred to as "it" but rather with the use of the personal pronouns "he" or "him."

Note

1. Harold W. Tribble, *Our Doctrine*, p. 59.

17

The Deity of the Holy Spirit

The Bible teaches that the Holy Spirit "is just as truly God as is Christ, and he is just as really present with us as was Christ with the disciples."[1] This seems to be in full accord with the words of Jesus who said to his disciples, "It is expedient for you that I go away; for if I go not away, the Comforter will not come unto you; but if I go, I will send him unto you" (John 16:7, ASV). This was to be a very special relationship. And again Jesus said, "I have yet many things to say unto you, but ye cannot bear them now. Howbeit when he, the Spirit of truth, is come, he shall guide you into all the truth: for he shall not speak from himself; but what things soever he shall hear, these shall he speak: and he shall declare unto you the things that are to come" (John 16:12-13, ASV).

In truth, wherever the Scriptures speak of the Spirit, they refer to him as a divine person—God. It was he who participated in the creation of the world (Gen. 1:2), and Job looked upon the Spirit of God as the One who created him and made him a living soul (Job 33:4, ASV).

In the commission which Jesus gave to his disciples, he included the Spirit along with himself and the Father in the trinity, saying, "into the name of the Father and of the Son and of the Holy Spirit" (Matt. 28:19, ASV).

Thus, many of the attributes of God are also attributes of the Holy Spirit.

Consider his omnipresence, as reflected in Psalm 139:7-10:

Whither shall I go from thy Spirit?
Or whither shall I flee from thy presence?
If I ascend up into heaven, thou art there:
If I make my bed in Sheol, behold, thou art there.
If I take the wings of the morning,
And dwell in the uttermost parts of the sea;
Even there shall thy hand lead me,
And thy right hand shall hold me.

The Holy Spirit is therefore everywhere. He is in no wise affected by space or matter or time or circumstance. The Holy Spirit is both spatial and interspatial. How well the psalmist expressed the comfort we feel in our relationship with the Holy Spirit!

The Spirit is ever present and working in the conversion of people: "For in one Spirit were we all baptized into one body, whether Jews or Greeks, whether bond or free; and were all made to drink of one Spirit" (1 Cor. 12:13, ASV).

The knowledge of the Spirit is limitless: "The Spirit searcheth all things, yea, the deep things of God. For who among men knoweth the things of a man, save the spirit of the man, which is in him? even so the things of God none knoweth, save the Spirit of God" (1 Cor. 2:10-11, ASV). Wisdom comes to the believer through the Holy Spirit.

It was the Spirit of God that "moved upon the face of the waters," in the beginning, when God created the heaven and the earth (Gen. 1:2). It was the Spirit of God that wrought the miraculous conception of the Christ Child (Luke 1:35).

Such also is the testimony of human experience.

In New Liberty, Kentucky, an elect woman of the church, widowed by the death of her beloved husband, told me of the awful trauma, emotional and psychological, that she experienced at the time of his death.

As she turned to leave the graveside following the interment, friends entreated her not to spend the night alone at home, for there were no children or other immediate members of the family to be with her and offer comfort. She replied, "But this is a battle that I must fight alone with the help of God. If I do not face my loneliness tonight, I will have to face it tomorrow night, and my sorrow will be just as great!"

Spending the night alone, she said, "I retired late in the evening, hoping that I would be able to sleep—if I stayed up late enough! But when I went to bed, I was utterly sleepless. I just lay there until the early hours of the morning, tossing upon my pillow, and crying, and thinking, 'How can I face these days ahead without my husband? How can I go on without his help, his presence?'

"Finally," she said, "I thought of God's words, 'Fear not . . . I will be with you.' And then I slipped out of my bed and knelt in prayer to my God, earnestly entreating the Lord to help me and to give me strength for the lonely days ahead."

Then, after a quiet pause she continued, "You may not be able to understand what I am going to share with you now, but as I knelt there by my bed begging God for his presence and help, I suddenly became aware of his presence. It was as though he were standing by my side, and I could feel, it seemed to me, the touch of his hand upon my shoulder as he said to me, 'My grace is sufficient for you.' Don't be afraid. As I was with Moses so I will be with you; I will not fail you or forsake you."

This has been, again and again, the experience of believers throughout the world as they have come to know the saving love of Jesus and his presence in the Spirit.

Note

1. Harold W. Tribble, *Our Doctrine*, p. 61.

18

The Spirit's Presence at Pentecost

The Spirit's presence at Pentecost was the direct fulfillment of the prophets of old as Peter made clear in his sermon (Acts 2:16-21). But the coming of the Spirit at Pentecost was more than the fulfillment of the prophecies of old. Jesus himself, on the night he was betrayed, said as he spoke to his disciples of his suffering, "I will pray the Father, and he shall give you another Comforter, that he may be with you forever" (John 14:16, ASV). Continuing, Jesus spoke with his disciples concerning the nature and work of the Holy Spirit and promised them that very soon they would experience the baptism of the Holy Spirit (Acts 1:5). He also told them that they would receive power for witnessing after the Holy Spirit had come upon them (v. 8).

In his account of Pentecost, Luke told us, "There came from heaven a sound as of the rushing of a mighty wind, and it filled all the house where they were sitting. And there appeared unto them tongues parting asunder, like as of fire; and it sat upon each one of them. And they were all filled with the Holy Spirit, and began to speak with other tongues, as the Spirit gave them utterance" (Acts 2:2-4, ASV). And there, on that grand occasion, every person present heard the gospel in his own tongue. By divine miracle those present heard the disciples speak in languages other than their own and without previous learning—and were able to understand their words.

The New Testament records at least three, maybe four, other occasions in which Christians spoke in tongues. The people who heard the gospel proclaimed by Peter in the house of Cornelius spoke in tongues (Acts 10:44-47; 11:15-17). The disciples of John at Ephesus spoke in tongues (Acts 19:6). The disciples at Corinth spoke in tongues (1 Cor. 14:1-33). But the tongues in Corinthians are quite different from the tongues in Acts. The tongues in Acts required no interpreter, for each one present, whatever his ethnic origin, heard the gospel in his own tongue. This is why Paul said, in speaking of the tongues at Corinth, "If any man speaketh in a tongue, let it be by two, or at the most three, and that in turn; and let one interpret" (1 Cor. 14:27).

Paul said that tongues are to be regarded as "a sign to unbelievers and were not to be exercised unless one was present who understood them and could translate them."[1] This restriction should give pause to those who propose to speak in tongues that are wholly unintelligible to all others.

Note

1. A. T. Robertson, *Word Pictures of the New Testament,* 3 (Nashville: Broadman Press, 1930), p. 22.

19

The Holy Spirit and the Bible

In speaking of the writings of the Old Testament, Peter said, "No prophecy ever came by the will of man: but men spoke from God, being moved by the Holy Spirit" (2 Pet. 1:21). Jesus spoke of the inspiration of the Spirit when he said to his disciples, "When he, the Spirit of truth, is come, he shall guide you into all the truth . . . he shall take [or receive] of mine, and shall declare [or show] it unto you" (John 16:13-14, ASV; see 14:26). And let us remember that the disciples to whom he spoke later became the authors of books which make up our New Testament.

The Holy Spirit is the final authority in aiding one to understand the Scriptures. "The natural man receiveth not the things of the Spirit of God: for they are foolishness unto him; and he cannot know them, because they are spiritually judged" (1 Cor. 2:14, ASV). The Holy Spirit is the interpreter of the Bible; but one can receive the aid of the Holy Spirit only in proportion as he is born of the Spirit and yielded to his will.

A beautiful illustration of the power and the presence of the Holy Spirit in conversion is seen in the experience of the Ethiopian eunuch (Acts 8:26-39). The Holy Spirit uses the Bible as an instrument of knowledge in convincing or convicting those who are unsaved. What is more, the Scriptures aid the believer in his growth in grace and in the wisdom of God.

20

The Mission of the Holy Spirit

Just as the deity of the Spirit and the personality of the Spirit are reflected clearly in the Bible accounts of his work, even so the work of the Spirit, as recorded in the Bible, reveals the mission of the Holy Spirit.

There are many facets to the mission of the Spirit, and one of them is that of *revelation*. God's message for human beings came by way of the Scriptures, given by God in revelation. "For no prophecy ever came by the will of man: but men spoke from God, being moved by the Holy Spirit" (2 Peter 1:21). This is why the prophets so often, in announcing their message, would say, "Thus saith the Lord." They laid no claim to the message as being their own. They regarded themselves merely as mouthpieces of God. This same spirit of revelation was manifest at Jesus' baptism when the Spirit of God came upon him in the form of a dove, thus setting him apart, with the approval of God, for his ministry on earth.

Another phase of revelation found expression in the recording of God's message as we find it in the Scriptures. The Spirit saw to it that a record was made and preserved. This is our doctrine of inspiration. He chose the men for the task, gave them the message, and then guided them in writing it. The Bible thus written has perfect unity, is relevant to all generations of people, and is the fountain of divine revelation with reference to both God and man. This is a basic reason why believers look upon the

Bible as the inspired Word of God and as an all-sufficient rule of both faith and practice.

But the Holy Spirit is seen at work not only in the revelation of God's message for mankind and in the recording of that message; the work of the Spirit is also seen in helping people to understand the message of the Scriptures. Jesus promised his disciples that the Holy Spirit, upon coming unto them, would guide them into all truth (see John 16:13). And we know that as we are taught by the Spirit and guided into truth, we shall bear good fruit, "for the fruit of the light is in all goodness and righteousness and truth" (Eph. 5:9, ASV).

The presence of the Holy Spirit in the life of the believer serves for him as a guarantee that his relationship with God is a valid relationship: "In whom you also, having heard the word of the truth, the gospel of your salvation, in whom also having believed (trusted) you were sealed with the Holy Spirit of the promise" (Eph. 1:13). The Holy Spirit of promise "is a pledge (surety) of our inheritance unto the ransoming of his (God's) possession unto the praise of his glory" (Eph. 1:14).[1]

In other words, the Holy Spirit declares that the believer's relationship with God in Christ Jesus is a valid one in which the *sealing* (see Eph. 1:13-14) serves as a down payment guaranteeing to the believer that the joys and the blessings that have come to him in Christ thus far are only a token of what is to come at the last day.

The Holy Spirit proclaims a guaranteed relationship that is eternal. Peter calls this relationship "an inheritance incorruptible, and undefiled, and that fadeth not away, reserved in heaven for you, who by the power of God are guarded through faith unto a salvation ready to be revealed in the last time" (1 Pet. 1:4-5, ASV). "There is therefore now no condemnation," said Paul, "to them that are in Christ Jesus. For the law of the Spirit of life in Christ Jesus made me free from the law of sin and of death" (Rom. 8:1-2, ASV). Moreover, the believer knows that those who "walk not after the flesh, but after the Spirit," experience the righteous fulfillment of the law. "For they that are after the flesh mind the things of the flesh; but they that are after the Spirit the things of the Spirit" (Rom. 8:4-5, ASV).

It is easier to understand the meaning of the Scriptures if one has a knowledge of the life and times of those who recorded the Scriptures and a thorough understanding of all biblical backgrounds as they relate to history, to philosophy, to psychology, and to the grammatical aspects of the languages in which the Scriptures were recorded. But all this, of itself, is not enough; one must have the inspiration and the guidance of the Holy Spirit if he is to fully lay hold of the truth of God's word. Mere human intellect, with all of the material aids of study, is not enough. The great interpreter is the Spirit.

What is more, the Holy Spirit works with both regenerate and unregenerate people. For those who have come to know him as Savior and Lord, he is Counselor and Friend. But for the unregenerate person, he convicts of sin and of righteousness and of judgment. "Of sin, because they believe not on me;" said Jesus, "of righteousness, because I go to the Father, and ye behold me no more; of judgment, because the prince of this world hath been judged" (John 16:9-11, ASV). The Holy Spirit, said Jesus, when he is come, "even the Spirit of truth, which proceedeth from the Father, he shall bear witness of me" (John 15:26, ASV).

The angel of annunciation that appeared unto Joseph in a dream said, "Fear not to take unto thee Mary thy wife: for that which is conceived in her is of the Holy Spirit. And she shall bring forth a son; and thou shalt call his name Jesus; for it is he that shall save his people from their sins" (Matt. 1:20-21, ASV).

The mission of Jesus was to "save his people from their sins" (Matt. 1:21); and no one can understand the real mission of Jesus, nor the character of Jesus, apart from an understanding of the character of sin.

It is impossible for a person to be saved, according to the teachings of Jesus, apart from the realization that he is a sinner and needs to repent and believe in the gospel.

For man himself cannot convict a sinner of his erring ways. Only the Holy Spirit can convict of sin, and of righteousness, and of judgment.

In his work with the redeemed, the Holy Spirit aids the believer in his prayer life, making "intercession for us with groanings which cannot be uttered" (Rom. 8:26, ASV). After all, we do not know how to pray as we ought, and this is why so often we long for the presence of Jesus to teach us how to pray, even as did the disciples of Jesus in the long ago, saying, "Lord, teach us to pray, even as John also taught his disciples" (Luke 11:1, ASV).

The Holy Spirit aids one in becoming better acquainted with Jesus, for the simple reason that Jesus is "the way, the truth, and the life," and has promised us that the Spirit "shall guide you into all the truth: for he shall not speak from himself; but what things soever he shall hear, these shall he speak: and he shall declare unto you the things that are to come" (John 16:13, ASV).

The Spirit serves as a guide for the children of God who are on mission for him. Paul told us, for instance, of how on his mission journey when they had gone "through the region of Phrygia and Galatia" they were "forbidden of the Holy Spirit to speak the word in Asia." He also told us that when they were come to Mysia, they "assayed to go into Bithynia; and the Spirit of Jesus suffered them not" (Acts 16:6-7, ASV). Then it was that a vision appeared to Paul in the night saying, "Come over into Macedonia, and help us" (Acts 16:9). When Paul had seen the vision, he and Silas headed for Macedonia, "concluding that God had called us to preach the gospel unto them" (Acts 16:9-10, ASV).

In speaking of the Spirit, Jesus said, "He shall testify of me" (John 15:26). And Paul said, "As many as are led by the Spirit of God, these are sons of God" (Rom. 8:14, ASV).

One of the great tragedies of the contemporary church lies in her casual neglect of the doctrine of the Holy Spirit. This doubtless accounts for the spiritual poverty of the lives of believers in relation to the enabling power of the Spirit and the joys that derive from his presence in the course of their daily walk.

Many believers throughout Christendom are apparently wary of the doctrine of the Holy Spirit. This could stem, in part, from the religious fanaticism of misguided zealots. But it also springs from a lack of understanding. And this is extremely unfortunate because of the vital role of the Holy Spirit in our salvation. Jesus made it clear, for instance, that only those who are "born of the Spirit" can see and enter into the kingdom of God. "That which is born of the flesh is flesh; and that which is born of the Spirit is spirit" (John 3:6, ASV).

John understood this spiritual birth and made it clear in his own words, saying, "He came unto his own, and they that were his own received him not. But as many as received him, to them gave he the right to become children of God, even to them that believe on his name: who were born, not of blood, nor of the will of the flesh, nor of the will of man, but of God" (John 1:11-13, ASV).

The miracle of regeneration is accomplished by the Holy Spirit, and this is the miracle of the ages. For by means of the second birth, we become spiritually alive, raised from the dead, having been "dead through your trespasses and sins" (Eph. 2:1, ASV). Moreover, in this new birth, the prophecy of Jeremiah is fulfilled, for in speaking of God's new covenant with men, he said, "I will put my law in their inward parts, and in their heart will I write it" (31:33, ASV).

Note

1. R. Paul Caudill, *Ephesians: A Translation with Notes* (Nashville: Broadman Press, 1979), p. 25.

21

The Holy Spirit and Conversion

Much is said in the Bible about conversion. The word as used in the New Testament *(epistrophe)* means a turning (to God) and comes from an older Greek word *(epistrepho)* used from the days of Homer down, and widely used in the Septuagint (the Greek version of the Old Testament) meaning to turn to. In the intransitive sense it means to turn, to turn oneself, as of the Gentiles "turned to the Lord" (Acts 9:35, ASV). The word is also used to mean to turn oneself about, turn back, as in Acts 16:18; to return, turn back, come back, as in Luke 2:20, Acts 15:36; and to turn oneself about, to turn around (Matt. 9:22; Mark 5:30; 8:33; John 21:20). In John 12:40 the idea seems to be to return to a better mind.

In Acts 15:3 the word *conversion* is used with reference to the turning of the Gentiles from idolatry to the true God.

In the Old Testament the psalmist spoke of the conversion of sinners: "Then will I teach transgressors thy ways; And sinners shall be converted unto thee" (51:13, ASV).

In Acts 15:3, Luke, in reporting the mission of Paul and Barnabas in Phoenicia and Samaria, spoke of "the conversion of the Gentiles," and Jesus in Matthew 18:3 said, "Verily I say unto you, Except ye turn [that is, experience conversion], and become as little children, ye shall in no wise enter into the kingdom of heaven" (AT).

In conversion, therefore, one experiences a revolutionary

148

change in his life-style—a turning—a turning from the old way to the new way which is of Christ even as Jesus said to Thomas, "I am the way, and the truth, and the life: no one cometh unto the Father, but by me" (John 14:6, ASV).

Human beings cannot convert themselves. It is somewhat like the experience of the man from whom went out the unclean spirit of which Jesus spoke (Matt. 12:43-45). When the unclean spirit decided to return to the house from which he had gone out, he found the place "empty, swept, and garnished," but in reality, it was ready for any spirit. Consequently, the evil spirit went out and brought with him "seven other spirits more evil than himself, and they enter in and dwell there: and the last state of that man becometh worse than the first" (ASV).

Conversion is the miraculous transformation that takes place in the mind and heart of a person as a result of the presence of the Holy Spirit and issues in that person's turning completely to God. Jesus told his disciples that it was necessary for him to go away so that the Comforter (Counselor) might come to them: "Nevertheless I tell you the truth: it is to your advantage that I go away, for if I do not go away, the Counselor will not come to you; but if I go, I will send him to you. And when he comes, he will convince the world concerning sin and righteousness and judgment" (John 16:7-8, RSV). Now the word translated "convince" here in the Revised Standard Version is an old word *(elegchō)* which means to reprove, rebuke, expose, show to be guilty. This is exactly what the Holy Spirit does, and this Spirit or Counselor alone can provide both the motivation for and the means of conversion which brings one into a saved estate. And this saved estate is "the gift of God; not of works, that no man should glory" (Eph. 2:8-9, ASV).

Before a person can experience conversion, he must realize that he is a sinner, that he has broken God's commandments and fallen short of God's glory (Rom. 3:23).

If one would reduce the theology of the New Testament to two words, it would likely be the words *sin* and *Savior.* One cannot truly know the Savior until he has come to realize the meaning of sin.

Unless one is convinced that he has "missed the mark" (for this is one of the meanings of the word *sin* in the New Testament), he is not aware of the fact that he has transgressed God's laws, for sin, said John, "is lawlessness" (1 John 3:4). The word John uses is the old word *anomia* which means especially, as here, "disobedience to the divine law," or "sin."

One of the reasons that it is so difficult to win people to the Savior is the fact that they are not convinced that they need the saving love of Christ. Filled with the sense of their own self-sufficiency, they cannot see the importance of abandoning their own life-styles in favor of the life-style of Jesus.

When a person becomes "convinced" that he is a sinner, and therefore lost to the ways of God and the promises of God, he sees himself in an awful state of being. He realizes that there is no hope for his ultimate joys in life and that there is only condemnation for him to face in death—a judgment that forever separates him from the presence of God and the joys of heaven.

Conversion, of course, can only take place as one experiences the new birth, for without the new birth one is neither able *to see* nor *to enter* into the kingdom of God.

This was the problem of Nicodemus, the Pharisee, who came to Jesus by night. He was satisfied that Jesus was a teacher who had come from God for he knew that no one is able to do the signs which Jesus had done apart from God's presence (John 3:1-2). This is why Jesus confronted Nicodemus with the necessity for the new birth, the birth from above, saying that except one be "born anew" [from above], he cannot *see* the kingdom of God. "Except one be born of water and the Spirit, he cannot *enter into* the kingdom of God" (v. 5, ASV).

Jesus made it clear to Nicodemus that if one is to be his follower, he must experience not only the *physical* birth but also the *spiritual* birth. Every follower of Jesus must be a twice-born person! He must be born of the *flesh* (*ek tes sarkos*—out of the realm of the flesh) and born of the *Spirit* (*ek tou Pneumatos*—out of the realm of the Spirit), even as Jesus said: "That which is born of the flesh is flesh; and that which is born of the Spirit is spirit" (v. 6, ASV).

No amount of human reasoning, or human resources, can bring about this holy transformation. It is the work of God and takes place only when a person recognizes his lost condition, becomes aware of God's presence, and responds to the working of the Spirit.

When Nicodemus heard the words of Jesus concerning the necessity for the new birth, he was confused, perplexed, and baffled. "How can a man be born when he is old?" said he. "Can he enter a second time into his mother's womb, and be born?" Nicodemus somehow failed to understand that Jesus was setting forth a new life principle, a process whereby God is capable of transforming the whole human race.

It is interesting also to note that in Jesus' reply to Nicodemus' puzzlement, he only said, "Marvel not that I said unto thee, Ye must be born anew. The wind bloweth where it will, and thou hearest the voice thereof, but knowest not whence it cometh, and whither it goeth: so is every one that is born of the Spirit" (John 3:7-8, ASV). Then Jesus went on to say to Nicodemus, "If I told you earthly things and ye believe not, how shall ye believe if I tell you heavenly things? . . . And as Moses lifted up the serpent in the wilderness, even so must the Son of man be lifted up; that whosoever believeth may in him have eternal life" (3:12-15, ASV).

Again and again, in witnessing to people, I have seen this miracle of conversion take place, and always it came to pass under the obvious working of the Holy Spirit. Human words of witness were only instruments of accommodation—they helped to set the frame of reference for the work of the Spirit.

This is how it worked in my own case. Let me tell the story, for it is one that is as fresh today in the pages of my memory as the day when the great transaction occurred under the influence of God's Spirit.

It was my privilege to grow up in a godly home, a home of two Christian parents whose lives were shining examples of the Christian tradition. Both Father and Mother were devoted church people, serving faithfully in the various avenues of opportunity in the little mountain church, the Traphill Baptist Church of Wilkes County, North Carolina.

Father and Mother were devout in their churchgoing. When relatives came to our house on Sunday morning, Mother would say to them, "We would be happy for you to go with us to church, but if you do not care to do so, the house is yours while we are gone." And that is how it was.

I cannot remember my first day at church, for I was an infant, a few weeks old, when that took place. Mother took her children to the church (as did other Christian mothers of the community) when they were babies. There was no nursery or Cradle Roll then. The nursery or Cradle Roll was the sanctuary, in the pew where the mother sat. Often the baby would lie on a pillow and would be nursed or fed as was necessary during the progress of the service.

Prior to my conversion, we all regularly went to church on Sunday. We attended the revival meetings and heard the exhortation of the preachers to the lost. I attended a Sunday School class when I was old enough to leave my mother and listen to "Miss Lula" (Mrs. J. S.) Kilby tell us about Jesus and his love for people. I remember the little picture cards that told the story of Jesus and his daily ministry among people.

But nothing in the way of conviction had ever taken hold of my heart. For instance, I never had any thoughts about sin. Above all things, I had never regarded myself as a sinner. The fact that I was living under the roof of my father and mother, whom I knew to be devout, godly people, was enough for me. I felt need of nothing more. I did not even associate churchgoing with my own spiritual welfare. I merely thought of myself as going because the family went!

Once when I was attending a revival at the local Methodist Church (being conducted in what was the old Fairview College building at Traphill), I stood up on a pew where I could see better as the hymn of invitation was being sung and the preacher was exhorting the lost.

In those days it was a common thing for those interested in the lost to single a person out back in the congregation and go and speak personally with him. Such a person came to me while I was standing up on the pew listening with rapt attention to the service that was in progress.

But the words of the person who came to me, seeking my conversion, had no effect upon me. In fact, it appeared to me to be a sort of "funny" thing that I would be singled out in such a way, for I felt no need of such persuasion—even though in early childhood I had seen young people and adults by the scores go forward professing faith in Jesus. I had seen them after they had gone forward turn around, face the congregation, and relate their experience, but such never impressed me. I had no feeling of desire for such an experience—nor awareness of my need for it.

Once when the Rev. A. B. Hayes was at our home speaking with my sister Clair (who was eight years older than I) about her own conversion, he upset me greatly. Brother Hayes asked her, among other things, if she would give her heart to Jesus. Upon hearing this, I fled from the "parlor," where the family was, to another room, sobbing. Mother quickly followed me, put her arm around me, and asked me why in the world I was crying when the minister was only trying to lead my sister to Jesus. I replied to her, "I don't want my sister to give herself to anyone!"

But one summer evening in 1915, there in the mountain home, the picture changed. A spiritual revolution began in my heart that was soon to transform my life. I hardly knew what was taking place, but I was deeply troubled and knew that I would never rest until the problem was solved.

In those days, we did not have the kind of conveniences in the home that the great majority of mountain homes have today. There was no bathroom inside the house, and no waterworks. Our baths were taken in washtubs, and often in tepid water— water that sometimes became cool before the bath was over. A bath was therefore something that we children dreaded. We wanted to stay away from the procedure as long as possible! Sometimes we had to be physically persuaded to take a bath.

One evening before my bath, I was lying across the foot of my father's and mother's bed. They slept on a mattress made of feathers (we called it a feather bed), and it was a pleasant place to lie down.

Previously I had been very ill with hepatitis. Dear old Doctor York, our family physician, called it "a torpid liver." I was gravely ill for days and days. In fact, my parents later confided to me that they were very apprehensive about my recovery. They had no drugs then to deal with the jaundice, and I lingered for a long time in that state. Finally I began to recover and was soon as good as new. But often I thought about how I could have died!

That evening as I lay across the foot of the bed of my father and mother, I began to have a strange experience. All I could think of was the illness that I had just had and what would have been the consequences had I not recovered. For the first time in my life I felt that I was a sinner and that I would have been lost, lost to God forever, lost in hell!

As I lay there and reasoned about the matter, I wondered how I came to have such thoughts? Where did they come from?

And then it dawned upon me that it was the Spirit of God that was brooding over me, endeavoring to make me understand that I was a sinner; that I had been a transgressor of God's law; that I had missed his mark; that I was, in short, a lost boy!

It was a soul-shaking, almost a soul-shattering, experience! I had never been troubled like this before. I knew that I had to have help, but I did not know how to get it.

It may seem strange to say it, but I shared the experience with no one. I told neither my father nor my mother about it. I did not mention it to my brothers or sisters. Rather, I withdrew and carried the matter in my mind and heart, troubled both by day and by night.

A little later the annual summer revival in the Traphill Baptist Church began, and I found myself interested in a revival meeting for the first time. I looked forward to the first service and went promptly and took my place in the congregation, not too far from the front.

At that time, invitations were not always given at the worship service. We might go months without an invitation being extended at the ordinary preaching services. In truth, I hardly knew there was any time at which one might be saved except during the time of the annual revival meeting!

In those days we had what was called "the mourner's bench," a bench at the front that was cleared as a place for those seeking salvation to kneel in prayer for forgiveness of their sins. At the hymn of invitation, those convicted and so moved would walk forward and kneel in front of the pew.

On the first night of the revival I went forward and knelt at the mourner's bench. On the second night I also went forward, and on the third night, and the fourth night, but to no avail. All the time I was wanting to be saved, but somehow I did not quite know how it was to come about, nor what I was to do in the process.

As I think back on it, I believe I was looking for some particular manifestation of God's presence. I knew the story of the apostle Paul's conviction on the Damascus road, and I think I must have been hoping to experience something of a supernatural order myself in order that I might have assurance that God was dealing with me and that I was responding to him properly.

On Friday night of the revival, as the last stanza of the last hymn of invitation was being sung, there flashed through my mind the words of Revelation 3:20 which I had learned in the class of my beloved Sunday School teacher, Mrs. J. S. Kilby—words which said to me: "Behold, I stand at the door and knock: if any man hear my voice and open the door, I will come in to him, and will sup with him, and he with me" (ASV).

Immediately I got up from my knees and went toward the pulpit where the Rev. Charles Cope, evangelist, was preaching. I gave him my hand, and said to him, "I want to be a Christian." Immediately the evangelist stopped his exhortation and asked me to turn around, face the people, and tell them of my experience.

At that time, I knew nothing about the theology of conversion. I knew very little about the Scriptures. I could not have offered an explanation of conversion to anyone, for such deep spiritual thinking was beyond me! I only knew then that God had moved in upon my mind and heart, as something from out in the faraway blue of the heavens, and that I had experienced a meeting with God—a presence that resulted in a transformation that would be a part of me to my dying day, and I knew that I would never turn back—never!

I knew, too, that I had a feeling of peace. I knew that Jesus had saved me. I felt that I would go to heaven when I die and that I would be with Jesus forever.

Shortly thereafter and before I was baptized, the family moved to Hays, North Carolina, so that we might have better school advantages, so my baptism was delayed until the cool weather had set in.

The place of baptism was a little stream of water where a dam had been made near the home of Mr. Pate Wood, down in the valley northeast of Hays.

Unfortunately, on Saturday night before the baptizing, the pond froze over. The ice was thick, but the Rev. A. B. Hayes who baptized me was not to be deterred by that. He called for an axe, and an opening was chopped in the ice so that the baptism could proceed. I almost froze as Brother Hayes led me and his son, Shirley, down into the icy waters. In fact, my clothes froze stiff as a board as we walked to the farmhouse, some distance away, to dress following baptism.

But never, in all of the intervening years, have I doubted, for one second, the genuineness of my conversion experience!

22

The Spirit's Abiding Presence

Jesus told his disciples that the Comforter whom he would send would abide with them forever: "And I will pray the Father, and he shall give you another Comforter, that he may be with you for ever, even the Spirit of truth: whom the world cannot receive; for it beholdeth him not, neither knoweth him: ye know him; for he abideth with you, and shall be in you" (John 14:16-17, ASV).

The physical body of the believer, said Paul, is the temple of the Holy Spirit (1 Cor. 6:19), for the Holy Spirit, as God's lasting gift to the Christian, takes up his abode in the believer's body and continues to dwell there.

23

Our Unseen Helper

The ancient Greek word *(paraclētos)* used in John 14:16 and translated "Comforter" in many of the familiar versions of the Bible, means "one called alongside" and conveys the additional idea of being "called alongside to help." In other words, the Holy Spirit is the believer's helper.

As the believer's helper, the greatest work of the Spirit is to glorify Jesus and make him the believer's friend and helper. Said Jesus, "He shall glorify me: for he shall take of mine, and shall declare it unto you" (John 16:14, ASV).

Paul spoke beautifully of this help in Romans 5:5b-8: "The love of God hath been shed abroad in our hearts through the Holy Spirit which was given unto us. For while we were yet weak, in due season Christ died for the ungodly. For scarcely for a righteous man will one die: for peradventure for the good man some one would even dare to die. But God commendeth his own love toward us, in that, while we were yet sinners, Christ died for us" (ASV).

24

Assurance of Our Salvation

Paul told us that the Holy Spirit places the seal of divine approval upon the Christian—even the seal of promise (Eph. 1:13). "For ye received not the spirit of bondage again unto fear; but ye received the spirit of adoption, whereby we cry, Abba, Father. The Spirit himself beareth witness with our spirit, that we are children of God" (Rom. 8:15-16, ASV).

Paul called this presence of the Spirit in our lives the "earnest of our inheritance" (Eph. 1:14, ASV), and emphasized the guaranteed relationship of believers with the heavenly Father—a relationship that will never pass away—and which is to experience its final, joyous realization in heaven at the last day!

25

Assistance in Prayer

The Christian, in moments of great depression when it seems that all is lost and even the very presence of God is hardly felt, need not despair, for Paul told us, "And in like manner the Spirit also helpeth our infirmity: for we know not how to pray as we ought; but the Spirit himself maketh intercession for us with groanings which cannot be uttered; and he that searcheth the hearts knoweth what is the mind of the Spirit, because he maketh intercession for the saints according to the will of God" (Rom. 8:26-27, ASV).

26

He Guides Us and Instructs Us

Jesus likewise promised his disciples that when the Holy Spirit was come he would "guide" them into all truth (John 16:13). And this is a promise not merely for the early disciples but rather for all believers of every age. Through his presence in our lives, the Holy Spirit enables us to grow in grace unto maturity, bearing the fruit of the Spirit, and this fruit, said Paul, "is love, joy, peace, longsuffering, kindness, goodness, faithfulness, meekness, self-control" (Gal. 5:22-23, ASV).

The Spirit, said Paul, can even raise people from the dead: "If the Spirit of him that raised up Jesus from the dead dwelleth in you, he that raised up Christ Jesus from the dead shall give life also to your mortal bodies through his Spirit that dwelleth in you" (Rom. 8:11, ASV).

27

Getting Acquainted with the Spirit

It seems almost incongruous for one to suggest that a believer needs to get acquainted with the Holy Spirit, but this is a very real need in the lives of many of Christ's followers.

Every child of God should be acquainted with the Spirit, for it is by "one Spirit" that we were "all baptized into one body, whether Jews or Greeks, whether bond or free; and were all made to drink of one Spirit" (1 Cor. 12:13).

The believer, in his new birth, is born of the Spirit, for Jesus, in his words to Nicodemus, made it indubitably clear that: "Except one be born of water and the Spirit," he can neither see nor enter into the kingdom of God. "That which is born of the flesh is flesh; and that which is born of the Spirit is spirit" (John 3:5-6, ASV). Jesus said here that every person must experience the new birth, if that person is to know him. Just as one is born out of his mother's womb, so one must be born out of the womb of the Spirit.

This new birth, this birth from above, is indeed full of mystery. But so is the wind and so are the rivers of the sea—rivers where one flows west and another east directly beneath it; "The wind bloweth where it will, and thou hearest the voice thereof, but knowest not whence it cometh, and whither it goeth: so is every one that is born of the Spirit" (John 3:8).

Surely we all need to know the Holy Spirit in a personal way, for how can our fellowship with the Lord be real unless we are acquainted with his Spirit? "For as many as are led by the Spirit of God," said Paul, "these are sons of God" (Rom. 8:14, ASV).

But how, you ask, may one be led of the Spirit?

We can be led by the Spirit as we study his Word, the Bible, and seek to understand its precepts.

We can be led by the Spirit as we tarry in the fellowship of the Spirit on the knees of prayer. Many of us have a shallow prayer experience. We lose sight of the example of our Savior whose prayer life was as constant as his days. We know that on at least one occasion "he went out into the mountain to pray; and he continued all night in prayer to God" (Luke 6:12). And on that particular occasion, he had no greater burden than that of choosing the twelve men whom he would call apostles.

For those who would become better acquainted with the Holy Spirit, let them spend much time not only in Bible study and in prayer but also in meditation. In such moments of quiet, one receives bright and moving intimations from the Spirit. And let us remember that what the Lord has to say to us is far more than any word we can utter to him in our spoken prayers.

Once again, one grows in his knowledge and understanding of the Holy Spirit through witnessing to the saving power of the risen Lord. "But ye shall receive power," said Jesus, "when the Holy Spirit is come upon you: and ye shall be my witnesses both in Jerusalem, and in all Judaea and Samaria, and unto the uttermost part of the earth" (Acts 1:8, ASV).

Finally, only those who are "led of the Spirit" (Gal. 5:18) and who seek earnestly to obey the commands of the Lord are the children of God and therefore able to experience the revelation of the Spirit and the fellowship of the Spirit.

Let every Christian, therefore, ask himself, *To what extent does the Holy Spirit have control of my life? In what measure do I experience his help in hours of need? Do I lean upon him for help when I pray? Do I look to him for guidance when I lose my way? Am I guilty of quenching the Spirit?* (1 Thess. 5:19). God is waiting to do abundantly more than we can think or ask if we as Christians will only yield our lives unto him completely and without reserve as faithful, devoted witnesses!